Author photograph © Renato Parada

PENGUIN BOOKS

THE FIRST READER

Luiz Schwarcz was born in São Paulo, Brazil, in 1956. He began his career as an editor at Brasiliense and later co-founded Companhia das Letras in 1986. In 2017, he received the London Book Fair Lifetime Achievement Award, and in 2024 he won the 2025 Cesare De Michelis International Award for Publishing. He is the author of the children's books *Minha vida de goleiro* (1999) and *Em busca do thesouro da juventude* (2003), the short story collections *Discurso sobre o capim* (2005) and *Linguagem de sinais* (2010), and the memoir *The Absent Moon* (2023).

Also by Luiz Schwarcz

The Absent Moon

The First Reader

On Writers and Editors

LUIZ SCHWARCZ

Translated by Alison Entrekin

PENGUIN BOOKS

PENGUIN BOOKS
An imprint of Penguin Random House LLC
1745 Broadway, New York, NY 10019
penguinrandomhouse.com

LIBRARY OF CONGRESS CATALOGING-IN-PUBLICATION DATA

Library of Congress Cataloging-in-Publication Data
Names: Schwarcz, Luiz author | Entrekin, Alison translator
Title: The first reader : on writers and editors / Luiz Schwarcz ;
translated by Alison Entrekin.
Other titles: Primeiro leitor English
Description: New York, NY : Penguin Books, 2026. |
Includes bibliographical references and index.
Identifiers: LCCN 2025048894 (print) | LCCN 2025048895 (ebook) |
ISBN 9798217062515 trade paperback | ISBN 9798217062522 ebook
Subjects: LCSH: Authors and publishers | Book editors | Books and reading |
Creation (Literary, artistic, etc.) | LCGFT: Essays
Classification: LCC PQ9698.429.C48 P7513 2026 (print) |
LCC PQ9698.429.C48 (ebook) | DDC 869.4/5—dc23/eng/20260106
LC record available at https://lccn.loc.gov/2025048894
LC ebook record available at https://lccn.loc.gov/2025048895

Originally published in Brazilian Portuguese, as *O primeiro leitor: Ensaio de memoria*, by Companhia das Letras, Sao Paulo.

Printed in the United States of America
1st Printing

The authorized representative in the EU for product safety and compliance is Penguin Random House Ireland, Morrison Chambers, 32 Nassau Street, Dublin D02 YH68, Ireland, https://eu-contact.penguin.ie.

For my colleagues and the writers
who invented my vocation.

For Lili, for everything.

Epigraphs are often used in literary and scientific texts and university theses, helping to enrich the content. Few, however, know their true purpose . . .

Federal University of Minas Gerais Law School website

CONTENTS

INTRODUCTION

The Last and the First

Back in 2018, when Brazil's two main bookstore chains were facing bankruptcy, I wrote a public letter, called "A Love Letter to Books," which was indeed a declaration of love, and a plea for others to declare their love for books too, at a difficult time for the publishing industry. When I first conceived of the book you are holding, I considered adapting that title. Given that the book is a series of dispatches on different subjects distilled from my career, it seemed to fit.

But as the work came together, "Love Letters to Books" came to feel a little too sweet and also too narrow. Yes, this book is an expression of my love for books, but it is also an expression of my love for authors, and for readers; there is a great deal of overlap between these subjects, but they are hardly the same. The book has given me an opportunity to think through the editor's relationship with these three entities—ideally and in all too messy reality. I alternate between sketches of particular authors and essays on more general themes. The separation between the chapters that deal with ideas and experiences is a way of organizing the volume, but ultimately they are all part of the same thing, since the sketches are infused with ideas, while experiences have always made me think.

The selection of profiles was based on two main criteria. First, I didn't want to talk about living Brazilian authors with whom I have an ongoing relationship. Choosing one writer over another who is still practicing his or her profession would be impossible and unfair. For this reason, I chose people who are no longer with us who played a significant role in my life and in that of my publishing house. Certain contemporary authors and figures are mentioned when they have to do with the profile in question, or because of their roles in specific situations.

The idea of the editor as first reader appears in several parts of this text, and reflects my desire to seek discretion in my personal and professional life. What a huge contradiction it is to write something memoiristic in nature, while standing by an existential principle that values silence and seclusion. I have tried to balance those priorities here, but I'm not sure if I have succeeded. Can a book, even if it is only partially memoir, be discreet and modest? Perhaps not, although I sought these qualities with all my might.

These fragmented memories of an editor are also, in so many ways, a collective history. Once—I think at one of Companhia das Letras's anniversary celebrations—I mentioned that everyone present was an editor: cleaning editors, sales editors, press editors, and so on. I wanted to emphasize the truly collaborative aspect of the profession, as well as to acknowledge the care given in every part of the book production line. As such, to represent all the colleagues I have been fortunate enough to work with in my professional life, in this book I mention only a few who no longer work with me. To all these great people and professionals, I offer my tribute and gratitude.

When I had chosen my title, a friend asked me, "Is it a tribute to Ricardo Piglia's book *The Last Reader*?"

Piglia was a good friend, and this particular book by the great Argentinean writer is one of my all-time favorites of those published by Companhia das Letras.[1] Nevertheless, the echo hadn't occurred to me. As I revived my memories of *The Last*

Reader, I realized that the title hearkened back to a beautiful image of Che Guevara reading in a tree, a respite from the persecution he was suffering in Bolivia. Literature existed, here, as a suspension of life, the opposite of war. But Che's "last read" didn't exactly take place in the tree, as real life moved toward a tragic end. It happened, says Piglia, in another situation, minutes before his death. The guerrilla had been shot in combat and taken to a classroom, where he was murdered. On the blackboard was the phrase "*Yo se leer*" (I know how to read).

Other images from Piglia's work struck me as particularly powerful. The first is a photograph of Jorge Luis Borges trying to read when he was already incapacitated by blindness; he holds the book close to his face, trying to decipher the words, his eyes practically touching the paper. The last reader is he who went blind from so much reading, along the way creating a world often described as a vast library.

Two other metaphors in Ricardo Piglia's book have Miguel de Cervantes's famous character, Quixote, as their protagonist. The first is the scene where Quixote, who loves to read, picks up pieces of paper from the street so he will never run out of reading material. Quixote reads everything and experiences everything. However, he doesn't read tales of chivalry in the story, except when poring over a novel about a false Quixote, by Avellaneda, which recounts adventures he never experienced.

Picking up papers to read later, or, in the end, reading a false novel about himself, Quixote is another *last reader*. There is also the case of Robinson Crusoe, who salvages a copy of the Bible and books in Portuguese—since he once lived in Brazil—from the remains of the shipwreck to take with him to the desert island.

This book of mine is much simpler. The profiles of these last readers, Borges, Quixote, Robinson Crusoe, and Che Guevara, written by a magnificent writer, give reading an epic dimension. What I've attempted here isn't nearly as grand. The last reader is, ultimately, a hero. The first reader is just an ordinary man.

1.

The Book of Chance

I often wonder how a person finds their vocation. At what point in our lives does destiny show its face? When does that part of our personal story begin to be drawn? Did I become an editor during my internship at the publishing house Brasiliense in the late 1970s, when I decided not to pursue my plan of becoming a professor of sociology, realizing I wouldn't find professional fulfillment as a mediocre follower of Michel Foucault? Or did it all begin much earlier, in elementary school, when I heard a short story read aloud by a teacher at Colégio Rio Branco? That day, the teacher interrupted his reading mid-story, snapped the book shut, and announced that he would read the rest in the next class. I couldn't do anything all afternoon, and that night I barely slept, my mind in the grips of the mystery. The next morning I learned that the title of the story was

"The New California," by Lima Barreto. It was a text that would later mark the beginning of my career as an editor.

I also believe that a health issue in the family during my childhood contributed to my professional destiny. For many years, my mother would spend her afternoons in bed, trying to maintain a string of pregnancies, which invariably ended in miscarriage. She had promised me siblings and my father many children, but they eluded her, one after another. Seeing my mother always in a horizontal position, whiling away the time reading novels, I imitated her, sitting cross-legged beside her with a book in my hands. Sometimes I interpret this habit of reading while caring for my mother as a prelude to my choice of profession. Reading and glancing sideways, concerned with protecting a loved one, is no ordinary act. *Reading* and *caring* are verbs that go together in the work of editing. I learned this lesson at a young age.

Chance plays a huge role in a publisher's professional decisions, just as it does in life. Professionals who boast about their feats tend to play down more imponderable factors, so present in our lives. Tooting one's horn instead of giving credit to others—or even to luck—is disrespectful, especially in the world of authors and books. A publisher's "incredible savvy" is often far less incredible than the lottery of encounters that literature affords us.

The first book printed in the Western world dates back to the fifteenth century. Gutenberg and his Bible is the best-known example of all, but Aldus Manutius—who lived in the fifteenth and sixteenth centuries and was Gutenberg's contemporary for a few years, though he outlived him—is considered by many to be the great pioneer of publishing. It was he who edited one of the earliest printed novels, *Poliphilo's Strife of Love in a Dream*, which, according to Adelphi Edizioni's legendary publisher Roberto Calasso, was the *Finnegans Wake* of its time. Calasso, using Manutius as an example, believed that editing is an artistic enterprise. Perhaps out of a well-founded awareness of his own genius, the Italian editor described the profession as an art. Once, we were both invited to a debate in Berlin on literary editing. Without knowing what the other was going to say, we presented opposing views on the subject. In his brilliant presentation, my colleague asserted that there is artistry in editing. He cited Manutius and Kafka's first editor, Kurt Wolff, as examples. With a much simpler thesis, I argued the opposite. To this day, I still think I am right. Please bear with me as I make my case.

First I'd like to share some stories from the early days of modern publishing, about a number of men and, unfortunately, very few women, mostly upper class, who decided to embrace the profession in the first quarter of the twentieth century—in many cases unconcerned with profit, blithely announcing that they would only publish books that appealed to their personal taste. This was the case with Alfred Knopf, a curious figure, as well known for his beautiful book covers as for his suits, impeccably cut but in colors that were a touch too bright. When he founded his publishing house, there were no mass-market paperback editions or book clubs, let alone digital reading devices. Books were set on metal Linotype, printed on nondigitized offset presses, and always stitched, never glued. There were no auctions or disputes between publishers over the acquisition of rights, not least because the manuscript would have to be completely retyped for there to be more than one copy. The publishing world was populated by upper-class gentlemen and, in keeping with the prejudices of the time, there were few women in management positions. If a Jew like Alfred Knopf wanted to rise to such a position, he would have to open his own publishing house. In the light of this fact, the apparent snobbery in the choice of Knopf's first titles says less about his personality and more about the anti-Semitism that was prevalent at the time, when many authors refused to be signed by a publisher of Jewish origin.[1]

Alfred Knopf's love of typography and sophisticated bookbinding, and the friendships of his wife, Blanche Knopf, with European authors such as Thomas Mann and Albert Camus, would lend the publishing house an aura of strength and pave the way for one of the most enduring imprints in publishing history. Blanche, who was initially Alfred's secretary, would prove crucial to the brand that bore her husband's name. Among her future contacts would be the Brazilian writers Jorge Amado, Gilberto Freyre, and Guimarães Rosa, whose books she would publish, not always in good translations. Blanche and Alfred's marriage, it's worth noting, wasn't as happy as their publishing partnership. Knopf was run for a century by just three men: Alfred Knopf, Robert Gottlieb, and Sonny Mehta, but today it is in the hands of Maya Mavjee, the first woman to head up the "house of the borzoi"—a slender dog that became the publisher's trademark but which featured only briefly in Alfred Knopf's life. The acclaimed publisher had no special love for the breed. Transformed into a logo, however, borzois remained forever in his life.

By coincidence, seven decades later, in 1986, when I founded Companhia das Letras, I made a statement very similar to Alfred Knopf's, unwittingly using the American publisher's motto to define the criteria for choosing the books that would make up our future catalog: "I will only publish books that I enjoy reading." I believed in this refrain, but, with time, I have consciously abandoned it. Unlike Knopf, I hoped to achieve acceptable sales results in the rather elitist Brazilian publishing industry of the late 1980s. I was criticized by one of the most important publishers of the time, Alfredo Machado, founder of Editora Record, who said, "Either this young man has very bad taste, or he's going to lose a lot of money."

Few of the major publishers of the time believed in the discernment and sophistication of our readers. Alfredo always treated me well, but he didn't spare me publicly. On another occasion, he said that I "laid eggs like a rooster and crowed like a hen." To this day, I'm not exactly sure what he meant, but it didn't stop us from being on friendly terms.

The reality of today's industry, however, is quite different from that of forty years ago. Nowadays, readers from less-privileged classes drive sales. In Brazil, this is due to fairer income distribution policies and initiatives to establish libraries and distribute books to the poor, both of which originated in the administrations of Fernando Henrique Cardoso, Luiz Inácio da Silva (Lula), and Dilma Rousseff, before the economic crisis began to be felt at the end of her first term, impacting on government book-related initiatives. A more diverse book market is a thing of beauty.

The outcry when we decided to publish more "commercial" books under separate imprints, aimed at young adults and adults, some of whom belong to classes with little access to higher education, came not only from outside but also from within Companhia das Letras.

It's good that we have broadened our scope beyond my original motto, and that a publishing house that largely grew through sound choices for a more elite readership now publishes books for all kinds of readers, always with editorial quality. I have changed my old refrain, a fact that still shocks many people, but it makes me proud. The move toward being a less elitist publisher, with books aimed not only at would-be highbrow readers, was an important decision, and it caused quite a stir. It has, in fact, proved crucial to the expansion of our business. It was an exercise that helped us understand how much we had to learn from those who don't usually frequent the circles of the so-called literary elite. Interestingly, many critics of the Companhia das Letras Group's creation of popular and commercial imprints were people who voted for or were even members of political parties that represent the working classes. Unfortunately, cultural elitism can go hand in hand with progressive political ideas.

Caio Graco Prado, my first boss at Editora Brasiliense in the 1970s, believed at the time that sending books to journalists was counterproductive. His assumption was that a person who read a review didn't need to read the book. They would have gleaned enough of a notion to be able to make a good impression on someone or look smart at a party with a summary of the text from a newspaper's cultural pages. This belief contained a good dose of prejudice against Brazilian readers. It didn't take long, however, for Caio to change his mind.

Before Companhia das Letras, other publishers already believed in readers' intelligence—houses such as Zahar and Nova Fronteira, and certainly Brasiliense in its new phase. At Companhia das Letras, we decided to take that faith to its ultimate conclusion, repeatedly showing our respect for our readers with every detail, including the book cover, paper, font size, text block, and line spacing. We made sure that consideration for the reader was present in every editorial decision, from the seemingly smallest to most important.

What happened in the United States and Europe in the early days of modern publishing was somewhat different from what took place in Brazil. In North America, the pioneering publishers were largely members of the elite, graduates from well-known universities, some of whom knew each other and even enjoyed a certain camaraderie. Bennett Cerf, one of the founders of Random House, tells this story in the delightful book *At Random*,[2] compiled from recordings he made for the Columbia Center for Oral History program, and published after his death in 1971.

Cerf, who was from a wealthy family, recounts how after graduating from Columbia University—the same university attended by Alfred Knopf—he took a job at Horace Liveright's publishing house, which was famous for having created the contemporary classics collection, Modern Library. Cerf describes the atmosphere in Liveright's office, with bottles of whiskey scattered about and sexual adventures after hours, in an era in which the lines between professionalism and revelry were blurred. Liveright, embroiled in all kinds of adventures, found himself insolvent and had to sell his best asset to Cerf, his independently wealthy employee. This was the first step toward the future creation of Random House, as Bennett Cerf and his partner Donald Klopfer decided, over time, that in addition to maintaining the collection of modern classics, they would also publish new books "at random." And they named their publishing house based on this proposition. Random House, now part of the world's largest publishing group—with which Companhia das Letras is also associated—was, in its origin, the House of Chance. The publisher's name certainly reflected its owners' dilettante intentions. But it might also unconsciously pay homage to the way the two partners met: While at university, they were random winners of tickets to a concert. They had never noticed each other before, but from that moment on, they became inseparable.

The beginnings of contemporary publishing in Brazil were perhaps not as elitist—at least in the sense that a good number of our publishers were not millionaire dilettantes. Here, everything began with a strong connection to the book market. Many publishing houses had their origins in bookstores; a number of great publishers of our time—such as José Olympio and Jorge Zahar—began their careers as booksellers. Others grew out of magazines that published essays of a political nature, such as Caio Prado Jr.'s *Brasiliense*, which later moved into bookselling. Despite being from a wealthy old-line family, Caio Prado Jr. didn't behave like a dilettante member of the Brazilian aristocracy. His habits weren't typical of the upper bourgeoisie; he was an intellectual devoted to the oppressed classes and was a member of the Brazilian Communist Party. (His son, Caio Graco Prado, had a greater appetite for life's earthly pleasures; some, perhaps unfairly, referred to him as a "left-wing playboy.")

Jorge Zahar is the best example I know, and perhaps one of the most beautiful. Born into a poor family, he was a voracious reader of French literature. The scene of young Jorge sitting beside his mother and reading Balzac's *Lily of the Valley* on a train as his family moved from Vitória to Rio de Janeiro is well known in Brazil. Jorge says he couldn't hold back his tears because of the book, not because of the long journey with his three siblings and mother, recently separated from their father, who stayed behind in Vitória. In Rio, Zahar worked as a street vendor and office boy for a goldsmith, until he eventually went to work with his brother, who had found a job in a bookstore and imported-book distributor owned by a Spanish anarchist. Years later, Zahar and his two brothers would set up their own bookstore and he would travel to Argentina in search of products to import, an activity that would later see him travel through many regions of Brazil. Zahar, however, was never strictly a merchant; he was always a publisher. His vocation came to him by chance, on the train that brought him to the city where he would settle and spend the rest of his life. His first mentor was Balzac.

Also curious is the case of Ênio Silveira, for decades an editor at Civilização Brasileira, an important house in Brazilian publishing history both for the quality of its publications and for revolutionizing the design of book covers, led by Eugênio Hirsch. Silveira and Civilização Brasileira were no less important for their role in resisting the darkest years of the dictatorship.

Silveira started out as a sociology student in São Paulo. Seeking financial independence, he went to work at his uncle's real estate agency. After his first major sale, he expected to receive the traditional commission, but was denied it due to the fact that he was new to the agency. A man of principle, he immediately quit the job. He then sought out Leonor Aguiar, a sophisticated woman, much older than himself, with whom he maintained a close relationship. Leonor offered to introduce him to her friend Monteiro Lobato, one of the founding partners of the publishing house Companhia Editora Nacional. Arriving at Leonor's house at the appointed time, the aspiring job seeker was shown to the bathroom, where the hostess was soaping and scrubbing the back of the legendary author of *Reinações de Narizinho* (The Arriving of Button Nose), who was in the bathtub. As he climbed out and reached for a towel, Lobato offered to introduce Ênio Silveira to his partner, Octalles Marcondes Ferreira, the chief executive of Companhia Editora Nacional. Octalles took a liking to the young man and hired him, later becoming the young editor's father-in-law. If Silveira's real estate agent uncle hadn't cheated him and if he hadn't witnessed the spectacle of Lobato in the bathtub, Civilização Brasileira might never have come to be.

Such stories sound exotic today. Although chance remains a part of publishing and bookselling, we live in an increasingly professional book industry, in which a good publisher can no longer begin without a well-defined editorial direction and clear understanding of the market. The publisher might even be named the House of Chance, after the coincidences that are at the heart of good literature and that bring readers and writers together. But their choices won't be like those of Cerf and Klopfer in the 1930s—casting about for books, initially luxury editions, to accompany the hugely profitable Modern Library.

There have been publishers like Roberto Calasso and Kurt Wolff—a member of the German elite, founder of the publishing house that bore his name, one of the most iconic in history—who believed that the editorial direction of their houses was the result of the keen personal taste of the publisher, in this case themselves. In this manner, a publishing house was a portrait of its owner, an erudite person who left his mark on each book, creating an absolutely subjective unity.

In my opinion, this is no longer enough—our times demand more than the vaunted "art" of brilliant editors. I hope new publishers always have a preestablished concept, a vision of the readers they want to reach, market awareness, and a visual identity—this last aspect was also very important for Calasso's Adelphi and Kurt Wolff. No less important is an awareness of publishers' social role in countries like Brazil. Even purely commercial houses should be concerned with this issue in their everyday functioning. They should also become acquainted with the latest marketing tools, including data analysis, a specter in the lives of those who believe solely in publishers' intuition. This way, armed with a coherence that will influence all of their actions, young publishers will cease to rely solely on their great creativity as founders of new ventures.

Companhia das Letras was conceived in this manner, as the antithesis of the primacy of genius intuition. I preferred to strive for professionalism and to recognize the existence of another dimension: that of the reader. Companhia das Letras came into being at a time when the whole book publishing chain started becoming fully professional, when marketing in publishing ceased to be a dirty word, when editorial practice revealed itself to be about attention to detail—the supremacy of that which seems small but is not. Today, one's financial foundations are also more important. When I started out, with $140,000—$100,000 from the sale of the apartment we lived in and $40,000 borrowed from my family—the competition was much smaller than it is today.

Starting a publishing house to compete with the big players may cost more now than it did in 1986. My goal, however, was never commercial importance; I hoped that by choosing well I could keep myself afloat with long-selling titles. Things turned out better than I had anticipated, and young publishers may repeat this story, only with the added difficulty of the number of competitors and books published daily. Nevertheless, small publishers have grown and are forging new directions in Brazilian publishing, creating a more democratic playing field. These new literary ventures offer alternatives to the usual ways of doing business, often operating with great conviction on an agenda of identity politics, carving out new and original paths, which the bigger publishers end up following.

To conclude this chapter, I will finish telling the story I left unfinished above. The sleepless night I spent when I was about eleven years old, after a teacher at Colégio Rio Branco read half of Lima Barreto's short story "The New California," ended up connecting with the beginning of my career. I joined Brasiliense as a business management intern. But as my love of books grew, I moved from management into editorial. As a gesture of respect by Caio Graco Prado—the first professional to see me as a potential editor—I was given a room with the desk once used by Monteiro Lobato, who, before my time, had left Companhia Editora Nacional to join Brasiliense. Behind me was a bookshelf, and on it sat a bound collection of the complete works of Lima Barreto, one of Brazil's most important writers of the early twentieth century.

I once suggested to Caio Graco that we invite a prestigious literary critic to organize a collection of Barreto's short stories. I've never forgotten finishing *The Sad End of Policarpo Quaresma* at Pacaembu Stadium, on the day I pledged my allegiance to the flag—an obligatory ceremony that all young men in Brazil must attend at the age of eighteen, whether they serve in the armed forces or not—while crying with rage at all forms of nationalism and military ritual. At the time, I didn't remember that the short story that haunted me for two days in elementary school had been written by the same author.

I made many invitations, but no academic was prepared to take on the mission. They were all embroiled in the absurd rivalry between Lima Barreto and Machado de Assis. And, without exception, they were rooting for the latter. So Caio, with his courage and irreverence, tasked me with putting together the collection myself. I was twenty-three years old at the time and didn't have a degree in literature, but as far as he was concerned, my appreciation for Lima Barreto and literature in general was enough. Reading the collection with the reddish covers that lived in my first office as an editor, I was moved to find "The New California." It was then that I realized that my life as an editor had truly begun that long-ago day at Colégio Rio Branco, with the sound of the book snapping shut and the teacher saying, "I'll read the rest tomorrow."

The New California: Stories was thus my first work as an editor. To this day, I still keep the copy signed by Caio Graco, which reads:

> *Luiz: This is the first of many books that you will edit. I hope they all reflect, as this one does, and as well, the care and love you have dedicated to it, both essential to creating beautiful things. I also want to express how wonderful and enjoyable our time together has been. With a warm hug from your friend and colleague, Caio Graco Prado.*

My own story as an editor, beginning at my school desk at age eleven, or on the edge of my mother's bed; that of my great idol

Jorge Zahar, on the seat of a train; and that of Ênio Silveira, caught between the greed of a real estate agent uncle and the unintentional sight of a peculiar bath, show that, when dealing with literature and human lives, the unforeseen will always play a fundamental role. Of course, there is a common thread running through all of these coincidences. Before them, in the lives of my teachers and colleagues, as well as in my own, there was already a foundation of unquestionable affection for the mysterious product we call a book. Even so, it takes detachment to recognize that there is something imponderable in creating a good publishing house without ever placing ourselves at the center of the action.

I wonder what other editors' starting points were—like reading a Balzac novel on a train seat, or the interrupted story heard by a mesmerized boy at a school desk? It would be fun to collect narratives like these and write a history of editing entitled "The Book of Chance."

2.

The Audacity of Dreams

I like to recall events and topics from my professional life as if I were in conversation with a young editor. It makes me feel that my reminiscing has a purpose or direction. As I reflect on my profession, I imagine my listener's curious face, reacting to what I say.

Much of my work today, in addition to participating in Companhia das Letras's strategic decisions and the general running of the business, is dedicated to assisting younger editors and staff members, answering their questions when called upon. And, most importantly, I read books in fields of interest to me, or by authors whose work I have always edited.

We have built a team of talented editors, whom I've tried to teach the importance of taking initiative and risks. In Companhia das Letras's early years, I didn't show this same attitude toward my colleagues. Always working in a manic state, too agitated and undermedicated, I resolved everything without thinking of the professional growth of those I worked with, without encouraging them to seek autonomy, or creating a richer future for all of the collaborators who shared the publishing house's fate with me. I insisted that my colleagues work independently, but didn't provide the preconditions for it.

At one point, I publicly repented in a post on the Companhia das Letras blog, saying I hadn't shown the generosity that both Caio Graco and my second mentor, Jorge Zahar, had shown me. At the time, I had trained the new professionals less than I could have. I oversaw their work without opening new doors, in a hurry to make decisions. Most of them were excellent editors in their own right, without any help from me. I responded to all kinds of queries, but I didn't offer new questions. Without exactly being authoritarian, I was centralizing, paternal, and peremptory, which is more or less the same thing.

A typical scene from my time at Brasiliense is a good illustration of how I began to share in the many small and sublime details of the life of a book, and, by comparison, how long it took me to learn to do the same at Companhia das Letras.

When I had been working at Brasiliense for a few months, Caio began making room for me in day-to-day editorial decisions. As a sign of his appreciation for my input, and because of the partnership that was forming, he began to call me into his office every time a new book arrived. On these occasions, Caio Graco—like Jorge Zahar—would sniff the books, a physical and symbolic act, to obtain a first response, through smell, to the long months of work that had gone into it. He felt, sensorially, that he had given form to something that was the result of his authors' enormous efforts. The tightly bound package of six copies would be delivered to his desk. When I came into the room, Caio would cut open the wrapping and take out a copy for himself and a copy for me.

The first time, I was surprised to see my boss, before even leafing through the new book, hold it to his nose and inhale deeply, opening it right in the middle, near the part where the glue that holds the pages together sticks out. Then he would sniff a random page, still giving off heat from the printer.

Having participated in this ritual, I began to imitate it, understanding that this was how we welcomed a book we had helped bring into the world. The smell really was nice, especially at a time when Brasiliense used glue, not stitching, to join the pages. At Companhia, for a long time we used only thread to join the sections that make up a book. Nowadays the glue is much better and has also become part of our repertoire, though to a lesser extent. Still, I acquired the habit of sniffing the first copies that came to me for my approval of the edition. I don't know if that

Brasiliense ritual influenced me forever, but new books, even those that aren't glued, have a special odor left over from the printing process and a particular kind of warmth. We receive this kind of child by sniffing it.

Perhaps this act, which seems of little importance, is not so insignificant after all. In my opinion, a fundamental characteristic of books is their unity. Or their integrity, in every sense of the word. When we sniff the glue or the stitching, we are sensorially experiencing something crucial to the existence of books: the fact that they are whole, integral.

During the writing process, a book is fragmented, made up of parts that don't yet know how they will become something coherent, unique. They are words, chapters, poems, paragraphs that exist only in themselves but that will take on a different meaning in the book, as they form part of a larger whole. They were written over a long period of time, in completely disparate moments, hours, and days, in which their author experienced a gamut of moods. The first job of an editor reading a manuscript is to assess whether what unites the text makes sense, if it is coherent, if the result has integrity, as there should be in the lives of people and institutions. A book that remains a collection of fragments and doesn't acquire a more general meaning doesn't deserve to be called a book.

It's curious that instinct is a quality generally attributed to editors. People say that so-and-so has "a good nose" when talking about certain professionals, often those who don't read, or read little, and instead "sniff out success" without wasting their time on pages and pages of originals. They make good editorial bets almost blindly.

I've already made it clear how much I disagree with this view of the editor's work, but the truth is that there are indeed cases of editors with "good noses." Bennett Cerf was one of them. He was educated at the best schools and universities, but his erudition was unsystematic. He wrote more than one book of jokes and was a panelist on the TV game show *What's My Line?* He was a likable storyteller with a charming personality. He wasn't a deep reader like Max Perkins, the editor at Scribner, where F. Scott Fitzgerald, Ernest Hemingway, and Thomas Wolfe were first published. Bennett Cerf's "nose" was undoubtedly present in the case of a very special book, James Joyce's *Ulysses*. I'll discuss the story of Perkins's relationship with his writers and Cerf's fight to publish *Ulysses* further along.

Allen Lane, who created the paperback in its modern format (pocket editions already existed in his time, but we owe the modern paperback to Lane), is another example of not only intuition, but also entrepreneurial verve and tenacity. He was the one who had the idea to found Penguin Books while waiting at St. David's railway station in Exeter for a train that was running late. He went to the newsstands to buy something simple to read on his trip and found nothing. He envisioned paperbacks in a format that would allow them to be sold in unusual places. When he got back to his office, he brainstormed the idea, looking for a symbol to mark the inexpensive books he wanted to publish and distribute throughout the world. He wanted a bird name, and his secretary suddenly remembered a penguin. Lane immediately sent his art director to the zoo to sketch the little creature, which has since become the most famous animal in publishing.

Lane sensed that in the Depression years—Penguin was founded in 1935—readers would want something affordable that fit in their pockets, with an attractive, modern look. The only way to make ends meet would be to have very high print runs and sales of at least 18,000 copies in the short term. Everyone told Lane it was nothing more than a pipe dream, and yet he quickly sold 63,500 copies of his first set of ten pocket editions to just one store. *Ariel*, André Maurois's biography of the English poet Percy Bysshe Shelley, was the imprint's first book. It was an immediate success.

The Book of Penguin, published in 2009 to celebrate the company's seventy-fifth anniversary, states unashamedly that Lane never finished the books he read, when he read them at all. Nevertheless, he transformed the lives of readers globally. His venture soon proved so international that he had to move the company's warehouse closer to London's Heathrow Airport to reduce export costs.

These brilliant ideas come from an entrepreneurial outlook that is more than one's talent for choosing books. I always find the notion of intuition misguided, focusing attention on the publisher's opportunism rather than the author's creativity. What determines a book's success? The brilliance of the writer's ideas and literary solutions, or the intuition of the person who "discovered" them? Finding good books is nothing more than a publisher's obligation; it's what we do. Brilliant books, on the other hand, are incredibly difficult to write and the merit belongs exclusively to their authors. Unfortunately, the only thing capable of surpassing writers' creativity is publishers' lack of modesty. A visit to the Frankfurt Book Fair, where book professionals from around the world meet annually for five days, is like a tour of the Hall of Mirrors at Versailles three or four centuries ago, where the French nobility would dance and observe themselves from a new angle every minute. For those who don't know how major international book fairs work: Thousands of publishers and literary agents gather in enormous pavilions, primarily to buy and sell the rights for works that will be published in the future. The fact that fairs bring together competitors in the same space, constantly crossing paths in the hallways or as they ride the escalators up and down, creates a hysterical atmosphere of competition, which those seeking to sell their authors' work at a high price take advantage of.

Business meetings and social encounters start at breakfast and continue until after dinner. Before the latter, there is the happy hour, when attendees jostle one another at the fair's most upscale hotels. At the London Book Fair, the same thing happens in the pubs near the pavilion.

The evenings are long—at times I've had to attend two dinners a night for several nights at the same fair, after sixteen or seventeen meetings a day. On top of that, some editors will pull all-nighters at parties or in the lobbies of trendy hotels. One year, I went to the Frankfurt Book Fair and stayed at the hotel where all the nightlife was. It was torture. I was young, already fairly well known in the industry, but very shy. Without the courage to invite colleagues out for dinner, and trying to avoid being invited to one myself, I ordered room service, alone, almost every night. Distraught at the thought of missing out on a great book, I would end up going down to the lobby, where the frenetic Frankfurt nightlife was happening. Feeling lost and phobic, I would head back up to my room and down to the lobby again, schizophrenically. I suffered in both places, wanting to be in one and thinking I should be in the other. I think I made the trip more than five times a night.

The narcissistic festivities of book fairs extend far beyond the lobby of the Frankfurter Hof. There are dances where publishers shake their intellects all night long, and drinking that goes on until some can't walk straight.

After nearly four decades of attending the Frankfurt Book Fair, I asked a night-owl friend how editors and agents like her were able to go out all night and return to the hotel almost in time for their first meeting of the day, over breakfast. She burst out laughing and, pointing to her nose, said, "No way, Luiz. Are you the only one who doesn't know how people do it?"

Caio Graco had the brilliant idea to launch *Primeiros passos* (First Steps), a collection of affordable primers on different subjects, beginning with political topics, aimed at young people, who were eager for access to knowledge after Brazil's long military dictatorship, during which time they had little exposure to culture in general. I was intensively involved in the editing of this series, which sold millions of copies in just a few years. We should remember him, Allen Lane, and so many others, who were often referred to as crazy, with a feeling of profound gratitude and appreciation, as well as take on board the countless lessons they left us. Their instincts were, without any exaggeration, incredibly well honed, but perhaps we'd be better off taking inspiration from the audacity of their dreams and their extraordinary obstinacy.

3.

Susan

In the car on my way to São Paulo International Airport, I couldn't get the thought out of my head: What if she asks me who publishes Camille Paglia in Brazil? When I bought the rights to *Sexual Personae*, by the pugnacious American cultural theorist, I had no idea that she had made a habit of attacking Susan Sontag, primarily for the purpose of self-promotion. The book had been suggested by a Companhia das Letras author and read by one of our editors. It had enjoyed reasonable success in the country, more due to the author's controversial profile than to the quality of her arguments. The thought tormented me. As with all kinds of paranoia, it was as if it was already happening. I cast about for what to say to Susan.

Because I had joined forces with the US embassy to invite her to Brazil, I was able to greet her right after she had cleared customs. It wasn't hard to spot her among the passengers jostling to retrieve their bags. Her traditional purple silk shirt and the white streak of hair at her forehead caught my eye. I approached her awkwardly and saw that Susan was surprised by my youth, as well as by the fact that I was there to help her retrieve her luggage from the carousel. I don't think five minutes had passed since I'd introduced myself when the dreaded question came:

"Luiz, is Camille Paglia published in Brazil? Who by?"

"Susan, before anything else, what is your favorite version of Beethoven's Piano Concerto No. 3? Mine is the one with Arturo Benedetti Michelangeli and the conductor Carlo Maria Giulini." That was my response, following my intuition. Even though I'd obsessed over just this question, I hadn't expected it so soon, nor had I decided how to answer it. But the tactic worked. I knew the essayist was a music lover like me, but I had no way of knowing that the version I mentioned was her favorite too. She quickly forgot the question about Camille, or sensed that this hapless editor was on her side. A coincidence of taste regarding such a special concerto was more than enough to erase my mistake of having published a book written by someone who bothered her so much. My error appeared to have been forgiven.

In the car, the conversation revolved around our shared obsession: searching for the best versions of our favorite pieces of music. As a result, at first we didn't talk about literature but a large number of sonatas, symphonies, and operas.

Before we got to the hotel, Susan asked me if there was a good music store in São Paulo. At the time, the best store for classical music was Musical Box, on Praça Vilaboim, which had a sizable selection of imported CDs, despite its limited space. There, Susan bought me a CD with Schubert's last sonata in one of her favorite versions and a box set with Janáček's opera *The Makropulos Affair.* Less than an hour after we met, I'd dodged the dreaded question and she was gifting me her favorite albums. Afterward, we ate feijoada and drank caipirinhas at the restaurant Dinho's in Jardins. That was when I discovered another of Susan's facets: her appetite, the apex of which I would witness in Rio de Janeiro at the all-you-can-eat restaurant Porcão, where she tried *cupim*, a cut of meat unknown in the United States, for the first time. The sight of such an elegant, remarkable intellectual eating *cupim* and licking her lips at a restaurant in Aterro do Flamengo was, to say the least, unexpected.

This set the tone for her first visit to Brazil. She had a busy schedule in São Paulo and Rio, but Susan's condition for undertaking the marathon was that I stay by her side the whole time. We truly did have great rapport, thanks to Ludwig van Beethoven, rapport that soon turned into possessiveness on her part.

The author of *Illness as Metaphor* and *On Photography* fell in love with São Paulo soon after the party that my wife, Lili, and I hosted for her at our home, attended by a large group of intellectuals, and assigned me the position of friend and local servant.

One of the guests was the literary critic Roberto Schwarz. I also remember that a number of important philosophers were present, including the Spinoza expert Marilena Chaui and Hannah Arendt's disciple Celso Lafer. Meeting Schwarz was one of Susan's three requirements for coming to Brazil. Although the reason for the trip was to promote her books, she accepted the tour as long as she could meet the renowned expert in Machado de Assis, in addition to the composer Caetano Veloso and the landscape architect Roberto Burle Marx. Susan had been one of the main champions of Machado de Assis in the United States, which is why the newspaper *Folha de S. Paulo* organized a debate between her and Roberto Schwarz a few days after the party.

I have never known a better reader than Susan. Her role in this area was as important as that of essayist and novelist. It was thanks in no small part to her that Roberto Bolaño, W. G. Sebald, Thomas Bernhard, Robert Walser, and Machado de Assis, among many others, were introduced to North American readers. And without Susan, French intellectual life would be much less known in the United States.

I myself became aware of Bolaño's work before other publishers thanks to her suggestion. Bernhard and Sebald had just been published here when I read them, also following her suggestion. I felt unbridled admiration for both writers and waited for an opportunity to publish them. Susan Sontag was the first to know when I acquired the rights to *By Night in Chile*, *The Loser*, and *Austerlitz*.

At the time, Bernardo Carvalho was still a reporter for *Illustrada*, the cultural supplement of *Folha de S. Paulo*, and was assigned to accompany Sontag to the favela Paraisópolis, among other places. There could have been no greater mismatch of temperaments than between Susan and the journalist who would go on to become one of Companhia das Letras's and Brazil's most important writers.

Sontag was perhaps the first international writer with whom I developed a close relationship. Before her visit, I had received other authors, notably Gore Vidal and John Updike. I maintained a long correspondence with the latter—interrupted for reasons I'll explain later. Updike refused to use fax and later the internet. His letters would arrive in delicate envelopes that he had sealed himself. Others who shared this habit were Don DeLillo and Bruce Chatwin. From Chatwin, I received a wildly fictional letter celebrating the release of *The Viceroy of Ouidah* in Brazil. In it, he claimed he had come to Brazil and been arrested in Recife by the dictatorship, and released with the help of the famous anthropologist and writer Gilberto Freyre. He spoke of his dream of ending his days dressed in a white suit and Panama hat on an old cocoa plantation in the south of Bahia, when he would finally have time to thoroughly explore the literature of his homeland. He also said he had a perfect sense of the universality of literature when he saw the window of a bookstore in the interior of Paraíba, with original editions of works by Oscar Wilde on display. None of this could be proven. The author of *In Patagonia* did have a reputation for spinning yarns.

With Gore Vidal, I committed every possible blunder of an inexperienced host. First, I trusted Alitalia to deliver the Rio–São Paulo tickets to Vidal and his companion, as their flight from Rome ended in Rio de Janeiro. The airline failed to do so. Luckily, I had asked a journalist friend of mine based in Rio to go to Galeão Airport early in the morning to see if the arrival of my distinguished guest and his partner was going smoothly. My friend helped as best he could, and the pair boarded a plane to São Paulo with new tickets purchased by Vidal himself.

I was waiting for them with Nelson Ascher, who represented *Folha de S. Paulo*, the American essayist's cohost along with the University of Campinas and Companhia das Letras, as the publishing house didn't have the funds to pay for the trip alone. We mistakenly waited for the writer in one wing, while he left through another. Minutes before Vidal arrived, Ascher had a panic attack and his blood pressure rose sharply, forcing him to go to the airport emergency room for treatment. After a while, I left him with the doctor and went looking for the author, who was pacing back and forth, fuming with rage, near the door to the domestic arrivals lobby.

I also had a hard time recognizing the writer, who weighed more than he appeared to in his publicity picture. During his stay, I noticed that he stood in profile and hid his double chin with his hand whenever he was photographed. Like many authors, he had his preferred angle. What followed was a succession of gaffes. I had asked *Folha de S. Paulo* not to send a car with the newspaper's name in bold letters on the door. I wanted something more discreet. They ignored me.

At the first party I organized for him, with the help of a social columnist, Gore Vidal was greeted in the living room of a mansion in the elegant neighborhood of Chácara Flora by a chamber ensemble, who played Villa-Lobos. At the University of Campinas a few days later, with the thermometer showing almost forty degrees Celsius and another chamber ensemble on standby, the author of *Empire* told me that if he heard Villa-Lobos one more time, he would flee the country. The quartet played Paganini, but to Vidal it all sounded like Villa-Lobos, whom he hated. Even worse was the sight of his mocking laughter when he came across the many paper reproductions of Renaissance paintings on every wall of the large room where they hosted the lunch for him.

When he arrived at his press conference, he teased the journalists, saying he had come to Brazil as an IMF envoy, as there was a rumor going around that the country was wasting money on literature. He also asserted, without any proof, that a Rembrandt at the São Paulo Museum of Art was a fake.

At the time, to the shame of Brazilians, the country had declared a moratorium on its debt payments, whose creditors included the IMF. No reporter laughed at the joke. At the *Folha de S. Paulo* event, Vidal made other jokes that two days later were criticized in the newspaper itself, in a scathing article written by his host, Nelson Ascher. That was all it took for Vidal to say he wouldn't participate in any more events with Ascher. Vidal was very paranoid and convinced that Ascher was an ally of his archrival Norman Podhoretz, who, like the journalist, was Jewish. The *Folha de S. Paulo* saw Vidal's decision as an act of interference with its journalistic autonomy, but it never occurred to them that they shouldn't have let their host be the critic of their guest's lectures. They could have maintained independence and cordiality at the same time by assigning different people to the two roles.

After several evenings of parties, I took Vidal and his companion to the country house of an upper-class Brazilian poet. I was told the place was nearby, but we had to drive for almost three hours, part of the way on a dirt road. I was driving my father's vehicle—I didn't think mine was up to the guest's standards—which featured the novelty of electric windows. Unsure how to operate them, halfway through the trip, I inadvertently pressed a button that closed the window on Vidal's arm, much to the dismay of his boyfriend, who cried for help in the back seat. At the party, the unsuspecting essayist sat in his only suit pants on a freshly painted green bench by the pool. To complicate matters, after the feijoada, a traditional Brazilian stew of black beans and pork, he didn't come out of the bathroom for a painfully long time.

At the next party, he asked me for "something for the nose," and I thought he had a cold! Not long afterward, he spotted a partygoer who had been at another reception and told me, "No worries, he'll know where to get what I want."

With Updike, an extremely kind and curious man, it was all much easier. His Brazilian dream was to see the Southern Cross. And that is what he did, in Rio de Janeiro, in very good company. He met Rubem Fonseca, João Ubaldo Ribeiro, Ana Miranda, Sérgio Sant'Anna, and a number of other celebrated authors at a party at the home of my partner in Companhia das Letras, Fernando Moreira Salles, in Flamengo, with a beautiful view across the bay to the neighborhood of Urca. He wanted to go to Brasília for a day. When he stepped into the somber Metropolitan Cathedral designed by Oscar Niemeyer, he told me, "Luiz, this is the ideal place for a Rubem Fonseca story."

Before that, when he got off his flight, he had complained that he'd been upgraded to first class and he wasn't used to all that luxury. Later, during lunch, he fell ill, nearly fainting in the bathroom at the restaurant Massimo. He blamed the luxury of the flight, but I thought it was our conversation about inflation that was to blame. Seeing my concern, Updike said he knew the symptoms of a heart attack—the hero of the book he'd come to launch in Brazil, Harry Angstrom, had died of one. He added that he was certain he wasn't suffering anything similar. He asked me to cut lunch short, as he wanted to go back to the hotel to rest. Once there, he insisted I leave him alone and go home. Before leaving, I asked the concierge not to let anyone go up to the writer's room until I returned a little later. I also left him the list of media outlets that would be interviewing Updike that afternoon. If I wasn't back in time, anyone not on the list was strictly forbidden to speak to him. When I returned, the same concierge proudly announced, "The TV Manchete crew is already upstairs." I raced up and found the author of *Rabbit, Run* holding two live rabbits by the ears and being filmed by a TV station that wasn't on the list. "Don't I look better now?" he asked me. Updike enjoyed his visit to Brazil so much that he decided to write a book with the country's name as the title. That's when our friendship cooled, as I had to make observations about the text's historical accuracy. He wasn't very happy about what I had to say. At one point, we discussed the book's realism, but in my view the problem wasn't the literary genre but chronological and geographical errors. He argued that he had written a text inspired by magic realism. However, tired of arguing, and to be courteous, he allowed me to participate in the corrections. I believe the book was the greatest flop of the gracious writer's career, and Updike never wanted to come to Brazil again.

Updike and Vidal's relationship with Brazil was very different from Susan's. Updike was drawn to the country for a while, then forgot about it. Vidal, after the gaffes in São Paulo, enjoyed himself in Rio, but as far as he was concerned, Brazil was just another stop in the constant touring of a globe-trotting writer. My relationship with the author of *Against Interpretation* ran deeper. Contrary to my hunch, Susan hated Rio de Janeiro and loved São Paulo, where she said she met intellectuals with reading habits and tastes similar to hers. In Rio, she fulfilled her two other Brazilian wishes. She dined with Caetano Veloso, with whom she became friends. (One of her last outings, before the relapse of the disease that killed her, was to attend a concert by the Bahian composer in New York. Ever since she had come to Brazil, she hadn't missed a single one.)

The trip to Burle Marx's farm, where he himself welcomed and showed us around, was emotionally intense. Susan learned that the modernist landscaper had designed sets and costumes for Wagner's *Parsifal*. Burle Marx showed her the sketches, and she immediately issued me an order: "Luiz, I've had good meetings here, but I really like São Paulo, where I want to live for a year. Just as I lived in Tokyo, Sarajevo, and Berlin, I want to live in your city. To do so, I need a project, and that project will be directing Wagner's opera at the Municipal Theater of São Paulo, with sets and costumes by Burle Marx. Make it happen for me."

She didn't notice, but I froze. I was already beginning to sense a deep friendship blossoming between us, and more than that, an alignment of literary and musical tastes. But with her possessiveness, it would be impossible to have her living nearby. Where would I find time for other authors and my family? Perhaps for this reason, I did nothing to bring to fruition the mission she had imposed on me, which was difficult in and of itself.

Susan came to Brazil a second time to promote her last novel, *In America*. But the pretext for her visit was an invitation from the National Library of Rio de Janeiro to participate in a debate with historian Carlo Ginzburg. Combining the National Library's initiative with her new book and desire to return here, we soon met again in Rio. The debate, moderated by my wife, Lili, herself a renowned historian, couldn't have been more catastrophic. There was no common language between an academic like Ginzburg and an activist and intellectual like Sontag, no matter how hard the mediator tried. Susan left the venue complaining about the hermeticism of her fellow panelist, who must have dismissed her speech as superficial compared to the kind of historiographical approach that he advocated for. However, the Italian historian didn't criticize the event. There was no need for it; his displeasure was evident in his expressions as she spoke.

After that, we saw each other a few times in New York, and Susan even asked about her Wagnerian project in São Paulo, but I think I changed the subject, as I had with the question about Camille Paglia. During these encounters, she usually took me to one of her favorite dining spots, always very original, like a ramen restaurant in the East Village whose main decor was a huge pasta machine that took up almost the entire space. (I tried to return after her death, but it wasn't there anymore.)

On one occasion, Susan heard that I'd been in New York and hadn't looked her up. She reacted furiously when she saw me a year later, but, as always, her anger quickly subsided.

Shortly before she died, I made a faux pas. I sent her a season's greetings card saying I was sure she'd be fine in the year to come and that I looked forward to seeing her again. I don't think Susan even saw my card, but it showed that I wasn't aware of the severity of her condition. She passed away on December 28, 2004.

On March 30 of the following year, a memorial service was held in a room at Carnegie Hall. Mitsuko Uchida, one of our favorite pianists and a close friend of Susan's, performed pieces by Beethoven and Schoenberg. I wonder if what she played was mentioned by Susan in the car, that time we drove from the international airport to São Paulo. In any case, I deeply regret not having taken the initiative to go to New York to participate in the tribute to an unforgettable intellectual and friend.

4.

Whose Book Is This?

We don't usually understand literature as a dialogue. Typically, when publishing professionals think of readers, they think they need to entice them to buy the book so they may have hours of pleasant or enriching cultural entertainment. The author's name is repeated ad nauseam: on the cover, on the spine, on the frontispiece, on the credits page, sometimes at the top of pages, and occasionally even in the epigraph, as if to remind the reader that the book "has a sole owner." The role of a more conventional epigraph, with a quote from another author's work, is to present the author's family tree; it shows readers where what they are about to read comes from, subtly pointing to the book's ancestry, introducing the text's forebearers. I have seen cases where an author takes an epigraph from their own work and doesn't cite the source; in this manner, they don't trace a line to their predecessors, but begin the book by navel-gazing.

A good or well-chosen epigraph speaks to the rest of the book, but when it's merely an exercise in narcissism, all it does is add gloss to the writer's biography, which is usually emblazoned across the inside flaps or on the back cover anyway.

Signposting the role of the author with all these markings is, to some extent, fair. It extols their artistic work, but it is also part of a culture that establishes the absolute primacy of writers in relation to readers—the same thing happens in other arts, with the artist occupying cameras, stages, daises, and walls. In this manner, readers and audiences aren't considered part of the work; they are simply passive consumers. But it's worth remembering that this wasn't always the case.

The lines of a silent power struggle between writer and readers are drawn in the book itself. Symbolically, during and after reading, one might rightfully ask: Whose book is this?

I've always been keen to find studies that investigate what leads something to emerge from a writer's memory and imagination and migrate to the pages of books, whether first written out by hand or composed on the blank page of a computer screen.

I dream of making a more systematic investigation of the psychology and neuroscience of artistic creation, to help me understand the inner workings of memory and its relationship to literary creation. I may not have the time to properly explore the subject until I retire, which would be somewhat cruel: I'll be better able to understand my trade once I've left it. I will read about the past of the practice to which I have dedicated my life as if I were a first-year student of literature or publishing, as if I were returning to the early days of my internship at Brasiliense—where I began without knowing anything about books, except that I loved them and couldn't live without them. This deep analytical knowledge will connect in my mind with so many memories of accompanying hundreds of authors in their creative process without ever daring to theorize about it. I don't believe that any kind of original, theoretical study is possible for me, as an editor. This is a profession in which we know a little about a lot of things, but never delve deeply into such a complex subject. An editor, no matter how learned, isn't a true scholar; we can't be experts in a range of subjects and scrutinize texts with extra-editorial, analytical authority. There are, of course, exceptions. In any case, what falls to us is a concern for readers, which is something we must take on at the beginning of our relationship with an author, relieving them of at least some of their apprehension about the reception of their work and its commercial fate.

That said, my first lesson in the meaning of writing came from reading Sigmund Freud's magnificent text "Creative Writers and Day-Dreaming."[1] In it, the Viennese psychoanalyst explains how writing is a form of fantasy or daydream that substitutes the play of childhood and is as serious and profound as a child's play. Both fantasy and daydream stand in opposition not to what is serious, but to what is real. So when a writer offers us his or her self, spread across multiple selves, they do so with literary rigor and technique, enabling us to transcend the barriers that separate us from so many other selves in everyday life. This and countless other masterful texts explain why Freud, quite rightly, received the city of Frankfurt's Goethe Prize.

As we mature, we lose our ability to play. We are orphaned, having lost the effective way that, from a tender age, we learned to counter reality. So we progress to daydreaming, our new form of adult play. In this manner, writing and fantasy relieves adults of the selfish flights of fancy that give rise to tension in our psyches. Hence the strong identification between author and reader in the coming together of fantasies and the pleasure generated by someone else's flight of fancy, which has the power to appease our guilt for this adult "play."

With this brief detour into Freudian theory, I am still far from understanding the unconscious realms of writing, but it's a good start. Until I am able to learn more about the deep mechanisms of the writer's psyche that underpin literary creation, I will concern myself with another enigma: how the memory of a book is formed, the memory that will stay with the reader. In this case, it's easy to conclude that what is absorbed from a fictional text depends as much on the innermost depths of the writer as of those who read it. This is because fictional texts awaken entirely personal resources of the imagination at both the moment of writing and the moment of reading. In this way, the book that remains etched in each reader's mind is unique to them.

But if the author's name is all over the place and the book is ultimately a construct of its dialogue with readers, where does this second protagonist materially enter the book? What marks would indicate the dialogue between these two fantasies? If the author is everywhere, where does the reader reside? Or, better, how is the clash between two imaginations represented graphically?

As I see it, the reader inhabits a book's blank spaces. The edges of pages, at the top, bottom, and sides—as well as the spaces between the lines, which we call *leading*—are the places that symbolize the reader's presence. The blank area, or the area not occupied by the author's work, has almost the same importance in a book as that occupied by the ink used to print the text. That's where the reader is. An oppressive, solid text block (the space occupied by the letters on a page) is, in addition to being ugly, inappropriate, because it indirectly suggests that ownership of the book, during and after reading, isn't shared. It peremptorily asserts that there is only one presence in the book: the author's.

Stingy line spacing states that the editor, with all his or her power, was incapable of recognizing that the place right beside what the writer says is where the reader's imagination stakes its claim. Lines that are too close together reinforce the author's supremacy, gracelessly.

The way a book has been handled, underlined, and annotated, as well as the creases in the corners of pages, are reminders of this dispute and of the reader's assertion of ownership that will remain forever on their bookshelves.

For the same reason, I believe a good book should begin with a blank page (or flyleaf), or with the title of the work alone, so that the reader has a place to put their name, their signature, or, as in times past, their bookplate, becoming the new owner of the text and, in this way, the author's neighbor.

I remember what we used to do with schoolbooks, in which we'd write our names so they wouldn't get lost on a school bench or in another classmate's backpack. Could this be where the habit of signing one of the front pages of a book after reading it, before putting it away on a shelf, comes from?

I believe that the reader's signature at the opening symbolizes many things and marks the dialogue, or the loving dispute, that begins on the very first line of a book and which can be expressed in infinite ways.

The blank page, available to the reader, resembles the blank page or screen that the author stares at before they begin to write a new story. These are demarcated spaces that harbor countless possibilities and contain the infinite, as if in a story by Jorge Luis Borges.

The first line of the text, the strokes that begin to fill the white background, mark a fundamental choice that will determine everything that flows from there. A choice that might begin like this: "As always, the writer awoke that morning full of questions . . ."

5.

His Majesty, Silence

In a memorable interview in *The Paris Review*, William Faulkner compares the profession of writer to that of screenwriter, always giving the former a clear advantage. Extending the comparison to literature and music, and even accepting the latter as the most natural expression of human nature, Faulkner reaffirms his explicit preference for words as an artistic form and means of communication: "I prefer silence to sound, and the image produced by words occurs in silence. That is, the thunder and the music of the prose take place in silence."[1]

In the excellent *A History of Opera: The Last Four Hundred Years*, Carolyn Abbate and Roger Parker show us how the pact between composer and operagoer is unrealistic from the outset. It would be silly to criticize opera for its implausible content. When we become involved with Violetta in *La Traviata* or

Brunhild in *The Ring of the Nibelung*, we enter a double fantasy, unrealistic by nature, since—outside of performance—life does not take place in song. When a story is sung, all possibility of naturalism is destroyed. Audience members know at all times that they are witnessing something that never took place, and don't fully imagine themselves in the place of the characters for the simple reason that they themselves wouldn't sing just seconds before dying or before poisoning their rival, not even to declare their everlasting love to the woman or man of their dreams—much less in front of a host of other characters, a conductor, dozens of musicians in an orchestra, and hundreds of audience members.

Those who criticize realistic or naturalistic literature should meditate on what Faulkner said, or on the fanciful nature of operas, whether conventional or contemporary. Life doesn't unfold in silence either. This is one of the weapons of fiction, unrealistic in nature, in which the author's and the reader's imaginations meet. Perhaps one could even say that literature is nothing more than the meeting of two silences separated in time—the writer's and the reader's. Paradoxically, it is silence that, in literature, opens up the path of fury. When reading a book, we are transported to the time chosen by the author. In it, we encounter emotions both subtle and overwhelming, original and unique in degree and nuance. Literature is an art form that rebels against realism, due to the high degree of subjectivity even in the most naturalistic narratives. Additionally, text can jump around in time and employ stream of consciousness and other narrative devices. There are also the interruptions provided by punctuation and chapter breaks. In real life, there are no chapters. Only in our imaginations. If we organize life by this criterion—which can only be done after the fact—we are all in a way, whether we are writers or not, making literature. Editors, on the other hand, must return to the silence that preceded writing, when the writer was staring at a blank page or screen, in order to better understand the fragility that is to be exposed and shared through the narrative. Another important point, and one that makes literature so different from theater or film, is that the author cannot control the way their book is read, including the pace at which it happens. Theater- or moviegoers take themselves to a location chosen by distributors and watch a performance in which the space for the imagination is contained—usually in the actors' facial expressions and tone of voice, the color of the sky on the backdrop or in the footage, and the set design that cordons off the imagination and tells the audience where to look. That's why Brecht was concerned with the alienation of the audience and advocated for theater punctuated by critical commentary, always reminding the audience that they are not part of the action. Nevertheless, the choice to identify with this or that character still belongs to readers, who always have the final say.

Fortunately, there are no set formulas in the world of fiction; some authors seek to influence our perception of their characters more emphatically, with which they risk banalizing their work. Others explore human ambiguity and leave doors open to the imagination.

Furthermore, a book isn't solely punctuated by commas, paragraphs, and chapters, but, above all, by the fact that readers decide when and where to read a book, and when to stop; their reading is punctuated with pauses, where they can include their own musings. In this sense, the rallying that began a few decades ago against realism in literature—which owes more to Tolstoy than to Virginia Woolf—is utter nonsense. All good literary influences are valid. They will never merely reproduce real life, nor are they likely to limit themselves to photographic realism. For this reason, we who enjoy literature must give thanks to the good God—the one who, as they say, dictated, whispered, or inspired the Bible, and who was, first and foremost, a remarkable writer—for the existence of so many literary genres.

I am obsessed with silence and so I seek it in the literature I love most. In the majority of cases, when I enjoy a book, it's because

I've found silence in what I've read. A silence that isn't my own. When a writer builds incomplete characters who are candidly fragile, or who have more doubt than certainty, I feel at home.

Without planning it, by pure luck, I found a profession that relies heavily on silence. Or, perhaps, it was the silence of books that pulled me in. The long solitude that marks literary practice lends a depth and sincerity to literature that not even the most fanciful of texts can avoid. The first time an editor reads an original, he or she must relate to the essence of the text and understand the foundations on which the book is built. At the heart of this process, they must encounter the author's subjectivity and seek narrative coherence in the smallest details. This is when they begin to fiercely defend the book, acting as the writer's double, protecting the work at all times, sometimes even from its creator. What is required of the editor at this moment is sensitivity and empathy.

Georges Simenon used to say he wrote to find himself through his characters. To write his novels, both those he called *romans durs*, which weren't strictly detective novels and had psychological depth and existentialist influences, and the shorter stories in his detective Maigret series, the Belgian writer would put himself in a character's shoes; he would stop thinking and acting like Georges Simenon for eleven days—the far too short period in which he would dedicate himself religiously to each of his books. He would isolate himself from everyday life, finish the book, and only then, exhausted, return to his daily existence. To understand himself and the world, in silence, he would transport himself, via fiction, into the soul of a character as complex as himself or even more so.

William Faulkner believed he wrote to free himself from dreams. The constant presence of a dream would distress him, and from that anguish his books were born. Writers don't emerge from literature unscathed; wittingly or unwittingly, fiction always leaves an intimate mark. In just these two accounts of literary work alone, we have categories that justify pages and pages written by those who set out to interpret the human spirit: the search for self-knowledge on the one hand, the influence of dreams on the other.

As I see it, by pouring their souls into their characters for many long months, writers unconsciously transfer their own fragility to them. This is literature's great feat: The vulnerability of writers and their characters meets the reader's vulnerability. This is why we love books, because they are the best mirror of our imperfection.

At the same time, we must bear in mind that fiction is a constant striving for perfect expression, leaving the author, after they have finished a book, with the feeling that their goal—

impossible by nature—was not achieved. The two writers mentioned above had something to say on the subject.[2]

> SIMENON:
> When a novel is finished, I always have the impression that I have not succeeded. . . . I want to try again. . . . Writing is not a profession, but a vocation of unhappiness. I don't think an artist can ever be happy.

> FAULKNER:
> If I could write all my work again, I am convinced that I would do it better, which is the healthiest condition for an artist. That's why he keeps on working, trying again; he believes each time that this time he will do it, bring it off. Of course he won't.

Marcílio França Castro, in his magnificent novel *O último dos copistas* (The last of the copyists), best defines what I'm trying to say here. The essay that opens the book states that "incompleteness is a literary genre."[3] Faulkner, Simenon, and many others would agree.

Many complain about the attitude of certain writers, allude to their narcissism, their demands for attention, so commonplace in our industry. These editors don't understand their role at all; in their error they pave the way for a dangerous conflict. They will pit their own ego against the writer's. They will confront books rather than comprehend them. By refusing to see how much vulnerability there is in the act of writing and making it public, they disregard the artist's needs, which are more than fair.

Narcissus delights in his own image when he sees it in a puddle of water, which serves as a mirror. But literature turns solitary creation into excruciating public exhibition. The artist is always a Narcissus who takes risks, dissatisfied with the delight that the mere projection of his own image offers him. From there, he presents his version of perfect expression, created in an ongoing search that is flawed by nature. By displaying, even if unconsciously, profound aspects of their personalities, writers can't help but feel insecure. And we don't always empathize with them and accept their vulnerabilities.

Publishing involves sharing with readers the solution that Simenon sought for his existential fears. Or using those same readers to free oneself from a dream, as Faulkner would have it.

For this reason, in the world of books, the only ego there is room for is that of writers—those who expose themselves through literature and assume the risks of doing so. As the Austrian thinker Karl Kraus said: "Artists have the right to be modest and the obligation to be vain."[4]

Furthermore, there is an ethical lesson in this incessant search for the perfect word that will no doubt never be found. The world would be better if societies cared about the shared expression of individual feelings. The lessons that come from good literature and other artistic forms are the result of striving for the best. What would the world of politics be like if this were understood?

6.

Amos

Is editing compatible with friendship? A professional relationship with so many moments of disparity, in which one side is always in a position of deserved reverence for the other—can a good, frank friendship be born of such a situation? As this book demonstrates, the answer is clearly yes. But sometimes it isn't. I take Amos Oz as the ultimate example of friendship between an author and his editor, and use him as a starting point to speak of the richness of my time with other great friends that my profession has given me. Amos, who taught me so much about human relationships. From whom I also learned how to recognize a great literary work, observing the most minute details that guarantee a unique portrait of the human soul. The Israeli writer's tenderness appeared in the smallest details of what he used to say. For example, the way he characterized writing as a pregnancy. That's the exact term he used. While writing a new novel or short stories, he would say, "I'm pregnant with a new book."

Of course, friendships with the Brazilian authors we've published from the outset tend to be deeper. There is a tremendous amount of dedication and devotion on both sides. There are also higher expectations and, as a result, opportunities for conflict. Not that there isn't a little of this in our relationship with foreign authors, but it's different in nature, in proportion.

I've made many friends in my professional life, not just with Brazilian writers. I dedicate myself intensely to them, developing relationships that go beyond the typical author-editor relationship. During the publishing process, we are in frequent contact, but even outside of it, when we don't see each other or talk regularly, the ties remain strong. The interludes have become more frequent due to my increasingly reclusive nature. But despite the long intervals, most of my friends are authors.

The writers I have hosted in Brazil, or with whom I established personal contact, not only in writing, have, for the most part, become more than just names in Companhia das Letras's catalog.

Because I can't talk about ongoing friendships with specific Brazilian writers, or choose one over another to discuss, I will focus here on Amos. Our fondness for each other was able to transcend the great geographical distance and long periods between one book and the next.

Curiously, it was his fellow countryman David Grossman who said the most beautiful thing about the bond we formed during the first of his short visits to Brazil. "Luiz, I feel so close to you that I only regret that we don't live in the same city, that I don't always have you nearby."

I'm sure Oz knew, as does Grossman, the story of the most iconic friendship between an editor and a writer: Carl Seelig and Robert Walser. Seelig, even though he didn't edit Walser's most successful books, took pity on the Austrian author, whose sister had had him committed to mental institutions after a suicide attempt. Walser was institutionalized for the rest of his life and received visits from Carl Seelig for nineteen years, after they got to know each other through letters. The two would take long walks and have deep conversations that resulted in the book *Walks with Walser.*[1]

It was due to Seelig that Walser's work, by that time forgotten, once again received the recognition it deserved. The day the publisher had to cancel a meeting because his dog was sick, the writer was found dead in the snow at a location far from the asylum like the ones he would walk to with Seelig.

Carl Seelig's dedication is an example of an editor's absolute devotion to a writer. After Walser's death, Seelig, with the help of two experts, deciphered the manuscripts Walser penned in the asylum, written in such a tiny hand that they were virtually incomprehensible. Seelig managed to decode and edit them, along with a five-volume compilation of Walser's complete works.

Let's return to Oz. He came to Brazil on four different occasions, and on each visit the time we spent together was special. The first time, he gave an unforgettable lecture at the Vitrine Cinema, which had been converted into a theater. Amos Oz, a giant of very small stature, spoke holding the microphone and pacing the platform. His height contrasted with the immense stage behind him. It had a red curtain, typical of old-time cinemas. The humor and tenderness that came through in his Hebrew-accented English mesmerized the audience. Everything he said sounded memorable: literary one-liners, anecdotes, philosophy, quotes from his favorite writers—especially Anton Chekhov and Israeli authors, his contemporaries. In my memory, they have become an enchanted collection of thoughts on literature in general and the Jewish soul in particular.

The next day, José Saramago, another of my best friends, and his wife, Pilar del Río, arrived in São Paulo. Lili and I organized a lunch at our house with Amos and his wife, Nily; José and Pilar; and Maria Emilia Bender, who edited both authors.

Amos and José were mutual admirers; they read each other's work. But they didn't share a common language, so I translated everything Saramago said into English, while everything Amos said in English was translated into Portuguese by Lili. In a magical moment, Saramago made an observation about time that was, word for word, what Amos had said in his lecture the previous day. There could have been no greater surprise—the literal coincidence of thoughts—to mark that ever-so-special lunch. Unfortunately, later on, a statement made by Saramago in Ramallah would put an end to his friendship with several progressive Israeli writers, who went on to sign a manifesto against the Portuguese author's comparison of Palestine and Auschwitz.

On that same trip, Amos and Nily decided to spend a day and a half in Rio de Janeiro. There, instead of visiting tourist attractions, they chose to visit the Casa do Pontal Museum, over an hour from the city center, which houses one of the finest collections of Brazilian folk art. Amos said that this would help him get to know the country better. He was right. Many years later, Saramago visited the same place and said he found the ending to his book *The Cave* while observing the objects on display there. He said that in that setting, he felt his book in a different way.

Amos's second visit was to attend the Paraty International

Literary Festival (FLIP), where he participated in one of the festival's most memorable events. He and his close friend Nadine Gordimer spoke for over an hour, without any need for a mediator. It was pure empathy, personal and literary. During the festival, Nily enchanted the streets of Paraty with her cheer, her instrument—the recorder—in hand.

During this visit, the Israeli writer was deeply moved to meet high school teachers in São Paulo who would go on to use his young adult novel, purchased by the state government in a massive print run, in the classroom. More than three hundred thousand children in public schools read *Suddenly in the Depths of the Forest*, which meant a lot to Amos and his relationship with Brazil. He'd certainly never sold as many books in one go as he did with that purchase for public schools.

The third visit was at our invitation, for Companhia das Letras's twenty-fifth anniversary celebration. Amos gave an inspired talk, over which the spirit of his idol, Anton Chekhov, hovered from beginning to end. The combination of quotes from the Russian writer with his own reflections ensured an hour of good humor and kindness.

The reason for his fourth stay in São Paulo was an invitation to give a paid lecture at a major conference, but the most memorable part of this visit—which Amos undertook after major knee surgery—was an event at a Jewish cultural center in the district of Bom Retiro. Upon entering the laid-back, charismatic space on Rua Três Rios, where generations of São Paulo's left-wing Jews have gathered and continue to do so to this day, Amos was moved by memories of newsrooms in Israel in the 1950s. He then captivated everyone with words full of humanity. He was enthusiastically applauded. On this occasion, he was walking with considerable difficulty, but he still made the trip on his own.

Our friendship also included two encounters in Tel Aviv. In the second, Amos showed me the manuscript he was working on and allowed me to take a photograph from a distance so no one could see what was written there. He, Paul Auster, and Milton Hatoum, among other great authors, wrote first drafts of their books by hand. Unfortunately, Amos never completed this one.

His cancer returned soon after our last encounter. At the time, Amos was more concerned with Nily's health than his own. Through the window, he showed me where he went for his walks at four o'clock in the morning, the time he usually rose and took a stroll to clear his mind and ready it for fiction. He said that when he walked through the neighborhood, not even the guards were awake. He would start writing in the wee hours of the morning and carry on until an hour before lunch. Then he would busy himself with Nily and other tasks that were less demanding than writing.

I also saw, in his hands, a handwritten page from one of Franz

Kafka's Hebrew lessons, which hung in a frame on his office wall. This I was able to photograph up close.

We spoke on the phone and exchanged emails regularly. In these conversations, we always concerned ourselves with everyone's health, since we were both clearly the *Yiddishe mames* of our families and cared for the Ozes and the Schwarczes with the typical exaggeration of Jewish mothers. It seems we took pride in this role, competing with each other to see who showed the greatest concern for his friend and friend's family. During our encounters, we would also roll out, in a thinly disguised contest, our repertoire of Jewish jokes. He always won, of course. The last time it happened was at a luncheon during his last visit, when the two Yiddish comedians dueled, with all the anecdotes they could remember, in the presence of President Fernando Henrique Cardoso, a great fan of the book *A Tale of Love and Darkness*. I was defeated without the right to appeal.

His death was a shock to me, something it took me months to digest.

As I said, I've experienced gestures of sincere friendship from various other foreign writers and publishing colleagues. I speak here only of those who live or lived outside of Brazil. Tomás Eloy Martínez was one who gave a lot in return for the editorial care and friendship he received from me. Alberto Manguel is a friend whose generosity knows no bounds to this day. At one point, I wondered why I had such close and special relationships with two Argentineans and two Israelis. But there's no generic or nationality-based explanation for such personal things. Tomás and Alberto were, as well as friends, the greatest supporters of my brief career as a short-story writer. Both threatened to publish my stories behind my back. They were better friends than they were literary critics. On one occasion, Tomás and I were strolling arm in arm through New York's Central Park when he told me of his intention to publish in an Argentine cultural supplement one of the stories I had shown him, whether I wanted him to or not. After that we went to an exhibition of Diane Arbus's photography at the Metropolitan Museum of Art.

I continued to visit Tomás at Rutgers, where he taught, and noticed the progression of the brain cancer that was rapidly taking hold of him. The last time we met on campus, he picked me up at the train station as he always did but had trouble recognizing me from the platform he was standing on. He seemed unsure of who he was looking for. I'm not even sure he remembered it was me he'd come to pick up. Tomás died in Argentina, having lived through some very sad personal moments during the course of the illness that displaced him from reality. Like Manguel, his kindness to me knew no bounds.

Alberto even published my two books of short stories in his literary collection at Actes Sud. He chose *Eloge de la coïncidence* as the French name for *Discurso sobre o capim*, a title in Portuguese that doesn't really work in other languages. He also wrote a wonderful introduction. The books were well received, perhaps as a result of the publisher's blessing, or the notoriously exotic taste of the French.

Another moment of extreme generosity that I cherish is an encounter with Kazuo Ishiguro, who asked to meet me when I became his editor, and then, inverting roles, proceeded to talk only about my children's book, *Minha vida de goleiro* (My life as a goalie), perhaps to make it clear that this was the beginning of a truly egalitarian friendship. Ish, as he is known to his friends, rattled off the members of Brazil's national team in several World Cups and wanted to know who my favorite goalkeepers were. Many years later, he invited me to the Nobel Prize ceremony, to which authors may take a limited number of editors. I had been to Stockholm once before, when José Saramago won. Editors love the lavish ceremony. Given the charisma and importance of the award, those in attendance cannot contain their happiness, gratitude, or vanity. The men wear a special tailcoat, rented online in advance, and the women wear gowns—the feeling that we are winning the award alongside the author is as pretentious as it is inevitable. Ish also spoke out, through his agent, when he learned that Companhia das Letras and I had personally taken a stand against Bolsonaro's likely election. On his own initiative, he expressed pride in his Brazilian publisher and asked that I be informed. The day before I received the Lifetime Achievement Award at the London Book Fair, he invited Sonny Mehta, his legendary editor in the United States, to dinner with Lili and me at a peculiar restaurant in the city. It was an elegant Russian restaurant, whose fame derived from the fact that the tables, surrounded by wooden paneling, had bells that allowed people to request that their champagne be topped up. Of course, Sonny, with his special generosity, refused to let anyone else pay for dinner.

I am certain that Sonny, who had previously received the same honor in London, was instrumental in my selection for the prestigious award. It was he, along with his wife, Gita, who played the role of host in the lobby of Stockholm's premier hotel when Ish won the Nobel. The editors attending the ceremony stayed up late, enjoying the cocktail party offered by Sonny, who was thrilled about the award given to one of his closest authors. I learned a lot from Sonny Mehta, never expecting to enjoy such close contact with an editor of his stature.

At a time when he was quite unhappy with his superior at

Random House, a major Brazilian publishing house was put up for sale and my partners considered buying it. The deal didn't go through, but I joked with Sonny that he could come to Brazil to run both publishing houses with me. Every time I visited New York, we would see each other, and he would say he wanted to throw a party so I could meet all my authors and friends. Being somewhat awkward and not much of a party person, I always declined.

Sonny's immense charisma stemmed from his discretion and silence. He was considered one of the most elegant men in New York, but he always wore the same outfit: jeans, a black turtleneck, a blue blazer, and delicate, high-end deck shoes. We were truly great friends. When Markus Dohle, then CEO of Penguin Random House, called me late one night, he prepared me before announcing Sonny's death. He spoke with Lili and then asked if I was sitting down, as he had some sad news to share. At Sonny's tributes, many mutual friends came to console me, given how close we were.

Salman Rushdie was another author with whom I became quite close. One day he called me to ask if I would like to accompany him to the 2006 World Cup in Germany. He had been awarded two tickets to the opening match, Brazil versus Croatia, when he gave an interview to a German sports program.

The irresistible invitation resulted in three memorable days with Salman. When we got there, we went to the monument honoring the Holocaust victims, where Salman was identified by a Brazilian television crew. Already averse to cameras, I confess that this time I hoped to be recognized alongside my friend, which didn't happen. We walked the streets of Berlin every day and had an unforgettable dinner with the Brazilian singer-songwriter and novelist Chico Buarque, who was in town for a concert and the game. Their birthdays are on the same day, and although they were already longtime friends, they didn't know it. June 19 was just around the corner, so we celebrated their birthdays early at Borchardt, one of Berlin's most charming restaurants. The night before, we had watched an awful match in which Brazil had won 1–0 but played terribly. In truth, the Brazilian team's performance hardly mattered.

Well before that trip, on his first visit to Brazil, Salman quickly broke with formality and opened up space for more personal conversations.

He agreed to hold the worldwide launch of his novel *Shalimar the Clown* at the FLIP literary festival. This feat should have made the cover of Brazil's most important magazines and cultural supplements. But there was an Islamist terrorist attack in London the week of the launch. The magazine *Veja*, in an initial interview, had mentioned the possibility of a cover story, but the attack got in the way. As a result, part of the media and most of the questions directed at Salman at the festival were about terrorism. He tried to protest at his event, unsuccessfully. Indeed, Salman has always been a wonderful human being, striving to be considered publicly as a great writer alone. As president of PEN America, he cofounded the PEN America World Voices Festival in New York, a goal as noble as it is thorny in a country as xenophobic as the United States. Many Brazilian authors were invited. Of them, the first was Chico Buarque, who spoke at the New York Public Library with Paul Auster.

I met with Paul and his wife, Siri Hustvedt, countless times, whether at their Brooklyn home or watching Paul edit one of his films in a SoHo studio. Paul's career as a screenwriter and director never earned him the same acclaim as his literature. But he was fascinated by the craft. Visiting him in SoHo with Lili, I could sense it. Afterward, the four of us had dinner at a diner in Greenwich Village. There couldn't have been a more New York setting for a meeting with the great writer. Sadly, Paul passed away prematurely due to lung cancer. An inveterate smoker, he was often seen with a hand-rolled cigarette between his tobacco-stained fingers.

Salman was the first foreign author to congratulate me on the victory of Lula, the 2022 Brazilian presidential candidate, for whom he had been rooting long before the knife attack that nearly took his life. I visited him at his home months after the attack, which occurred in upstate New York and left him blind in one eye, in addition to causing numerous other physical injuries. At the time, he described all the aftereffects of the attack to me. The loss of his will to live and good humor were not among them.

With Ian McEwan and his wife, Annalena McAfee, I had a wonderful time on a couples' tour of the Inhotim Institute—a huge, open-air museum housing large-scale works by Brazilian and international artists—and the old colonial towns of Minas Gerais, famous for their Baroque architecture. Ian wasn't particularly appreciative of Baroque art, due to its religious content, nor the very contemporary art of the Inhotim. But the trip was a delight due to the presence of Deborah Rogers, an English literary agent with a brilliant career and a list of several generations of stellar authors, above all novelists, of whom Ian was one. Deb was one of the greatest friends I've ever had. In addition to her and her husband, another notable figure was present: Jonathan Galassi, the renowned editor of Farrar, Straus and

Giroux. We all left Paraty on a rickety plane I'd hired. As I boarded the plane, I worried about my foolishness.

One night in Ouro Preto, while we were in a public square watching a show by the band Velha Guarda da Portela, a very drunk man asked Deborah to dance. The long samba between the man from Ouro Preto and the woman from London was a highlight of the trip, which also included a requiem by a regional composer in a church in São João del Rei, which we watched from the bell tower, in the narrow space between two bells. Jonathan, a poetry lover and poet himself, was above all eager to visit Elizabeth Bishop's house in Ouro Preto. We really enjoyed our visit to the residence, where the poet's charisma was still very present. On his return to New York, Jonathan tried to secure funding to transform the house into a center for poetry and translation. It was to no avail.

Almost two years after coming to Brazil, Deb had a heart attack while parking her car in front of her house and died instantly. A neighbor found her slumped over the steering wheel. It was a tragedy. Five years after that trip, Ian left the English countryside, where he lives, to present the award I won at the London Book Fair in 2017. The publishing industry can be quite unprofessional in many ways. One example is this: The Lifetime Achievement Award winner, not the awarding institution, is the one who must invite the person who will present the award and honor the recipient with a speech. I spent days of the utmost shame and anxiety after asking Ian's agent to invite him. I think I wrote to Peter Straus, who was running the agency after Deb's death, about three times, practically urging the author not to accept. Luckily, he didn't listen. Situations like this are common. Often, in other countries, when publishing a book, the author is tasked with soliciting favorable quotes or blurbs to appear on the back cover. In the case of my book on depression, published in 2021 and translated into several languages, I refused to do this.

Andrew Solomon is more than a good friend. Due to one of those incomprehensible publishing blunders, I missed the opportunity to be the first to launch *The Noonday Demon* in Brazil, one of the best books ever written on the subject of depression. Later, the book would be published by Companhia das Letras, along with Andrew's entire body of work.

Andrew and I both suffer from depression. When I was first invited to his elegant residence in the New York neighborhood of Chelsea, the topic quickly brought us together. For a few years now, he has been among my closest friends, frequently inviting me to dinners and lunches at his home each time I visit New York. On many of these occasions, he encouraged me, with subtle insistence, to write a personal account of my condition, in addition to acting as a counselor on the illness, which rears its head from time to time. He insisted that I check my medication with his psychiatrist and offered his house to celebrate the publication of *The Absent Moon: A Memoir of a Short Childhood and a Long Depression*, the title of my book in English. When it was published, Andrew wanted to throw a big party, which I was too embarrassed to accept. He wrote praise for the book that was printed on the back cover, which I read whenever I lose confidence in my writing skills. He interviewed me for the launch of the North American edition, a gesture typical of his generosity.

Robert Darnton—an important American historian, known for his literary talents and innovative historiographical examination of everyday life in different periods of the French Enlightenment—is a similar case to Amos. He became our friend when he was brought to Brazil by the cultural department of the United States consulate. On Sunday, we went to Ibirapuera Park to kick a ball around with my son, Pedro, who was still very young at the time. Afterward, we had lunch together at a steak house and watched the soccer match at Morumbi Stadium, where Brazil beat Venezuela 6–0. On the way home, we stopped at a kiosk and drank some fresh coconut water, very sweet and ice cold. Early in the evening, we picked up Lili and, without tickets, headed to the music venue Palace to try to get into a Caetano Veloso concert. We managed to get three excellent seats through a journalist who recognized me. As we drove him back to the hotel, Bob said that it had been the best day of his life, after his wedding.

Besides Deborah Rogers, I became close friends with Carol Brown Janeway, the foreign rights director of Knopf. The relationship between publishers and rights managers isn't always peaceful. Battles at auctions over works with high sales potential sometimes drive us apart. However, with Deb and Carol, true friendships arose out of professional contact. Carol heard about me when her assistant mentioned that a young man who was opening a new publishing house in Brazil wanted to buy—out of Knopf's entire list—only the rights to a collection of poems by Wallace Stevens. Carol wanted to know who this young man was who, according to her, had money to throw away. Luckily, she was wrong. The anthology, translated by Paulo Henriques Britto, sold well and is in our catalog to this day.

Carol Brown Janeway used to choose a select group of editors in various countries, all men, to whom she would preferentially offer her books. I was one of them. Always wearing a puffy blue dress that hung well below her knees, made up to give her fair skin a healthy glow, and clutching a black handbag, she would walk the corridors of the Frankfurt Book Fair, determined, barely glancing to the side. Carol was a mine of information about books from other publishers and agencies, and she enjoyed sharing it with us. That's how I learned about Sándor Márai, among others. Carol was the only rights manager I ever met who, in addition to handling rights sales, also acquired licenses, edited, and translated some of the books she commissioned, combining her work as rights manager with that of editor.

On one occasion, she decided to visit Brazil. She came accompanied by Maria Campbell, a scout for Companhia das Letras in New York, and her husband, Woody Campbell. Maria is one of the greatest friends I've ever made. Besides my family and very few friends, she was the only person who closely followed my major depression in 1993. A scout's job is to inform their clients firsthand about upcoming books, both in their country and worldwide. They represent only one publisher in each market and are always in fierce competition with their peers. Amid this hectic work routine, Maria came to Brazil several times and gave me the nickname "Concierge," as I meticulously organized our tours around the country. At the time Carol came to Brazil, Knopf had recently bought the rights to Caetano Veloso's memoir, *Tropical Truth*. They had also published Chico Buarque's novel *Turbulence* through its imprint Pantheon. I don't know how I managed it or what was going through my mind, but I organized a dinner in Rio for Carol, Maria, and Woody with the two singer-songwriters. Carol knew nothing about the genre of Brazilian popular music known as MPB; she used to attend a Schubert song festival every year with her good friend Ravi Mirchandani, with whom I am also very close. I always used to invite her to accompany me to operas and concerts in New York. When we left the dinner, which was wonderful despite the unusual group, Woody Campbell, still in the taxi, asked our friend from Knopf, "Carol, do you have any idea who you had dinner with tonight? It's as if you just spent a few hours with John Lennon and Bob Dylan!"

It's worth recounting one final episode of mine with Carol. When she won the prestigious Ottaway Award, she asked me to deliver the introductory speech on the night she received the award. I was honored. It just so happened that I had a ridiculous idea, and my speech, instead of focusing exclusively on Carol, began with part of a short story of mine in which a businessman who had won a marketing award didn't talk about his achievements, but instead digressed at length about a painting from his important collection, in which a blade of grass sprouted on a tropical beach. My intention was to show that literature somehow emerges from unexpected, random components. No one understood that it was fiction, and after the speech, several people came up to me to ask if my friend was okay. My intentions with that metaphor now strike me as incomprehensible. After the pseudoliterary introduction, I heaped praise on my friend, who I think, in the end, was happy, or at least she didn't give any indication that she was embarrassed by my childish opening.

There isn't enough room here to cover every friendship. I mention those that in some way mirror my relationship with my dear Amos. Each one is, however, unique and incomparable.

The opposite is also quite common. Fraternalism that never develops, where publishing is merely a business or partnership. There are worse cases, ones that end in enormous feelings of ingratitude, whether on the part of the editor or their writers.

Almost always, the announcement of the Nobel Prize in Literature takes place around the time of the Frankfurt Book Fair. While Amos was still alive, I would go every year to his agent Deborah Owen's little stand to root for our good friend. On one occasion, he came very close to winning. The Swedish Academy even consulted Oz's French publisher, to whom he was very close, the day before to find out where the author would be at the time of the traditional announcement. This publisher told me in confidence about the phone call, but when the award was announced, it went to Doris Lessing instead of Amos. With all due respect to the wonderful British author, I was deeply saddened. The Israeli writer, on the other hand, never believed he would be given the prize. He used to say that in more recent times, the Swedish Academy would never give the award to someone from the State of Israel, even if they were a pacifist.

When there's friendship, affection, or warmth of some kind in editorial work, life is much better. It's wonderful when we find in our authors the greatness that emanates from their literature. And when we, in return, have the integrity to treat their work appropriately. (The same is true, as I've shown elsewhere, of our relationships with other professionals.)

Amos gave me all this and much more. His writing emanated warmth and human greatness, which he, with uncommon generosity, brought into our friendship and time spent together.

7.

How It All Begins

It was yet another scorching afternoon and the pile of manuscripts, which should have dwindled or even disappeared—only to grow again with the daily arrival of new packages in the mail—seemed to be forever the same size. Was it the heat or his exhaustion from reading so many manuscripts, which never stopped arriving? In the tiny room behind the printing company his grandfather had founded, the editor would read the first paragraph of each book manuscript and dab his forehead with a handkerchief. That paragraph was enough. He knew whether or not to read on simply by analyzing those first lines. One paragraph, and the book in question could be discarded, like the sweat he wiped from his face.

The paragraph above could have been the beginning of a novel. My first attempt at writing a long fictional narrative was frustrated, like every one that followed. It really did begin like that. Then the narrator invented a series of openings for fake novels that the editor would receive and reject after reading a single paragraph. It goes without saying that the novel was intended to be a satire of the publishing world. Its plot would extend all the way to the Frankfurt Book Fair, the temple of the publishing industry, to which the jaded publisher would take excerpts of a nonexistent novel that he had written, along with fabricated reviews, bogus bestseller lists, and a bunch of other fibs—all the result of his displeasure with the direction his professional life was taking. The prank worked: The rights to the fake book, dreamed up in accordance with the latest trends in publishing, were sold to a dozen countries, and the editor found himself in a dilemma. He had to return to Brazil and actually write a book, for which he only had the idea and the excerpts used to sell the rights. To make matters worse, he was an editor, tired of his profession, not a talented writer.

Thankfully, my critical sense stopped me from going ahead with the project. But at least it provided me with an opening for this chapter, in which I will discuss book beginnings and a handful of exemplary first paragraphs.

What does a writer need to begin a book? As you can imagine, there's no consensus. Dorothy Parker would say that all she needed was a commission. Dorothy, like a writer very different from her, Louis-Ferdinand Céline, wasn't ashamed to say she wrote for money; in fact, they both stated that they hated the craft and asked themselves the same question: If not for money, why would anyone choose such an arduous profession? But is it true that they felt such contempt for what they did? We'll never know. We can't always put faith in what writers say, especially in interviews.

After receiving a commission, Dorothy Parker said, she would spend a considerable amount of time thinking about the short story in its entirety before writing it. She claimed that she found her characters' names in the phone book and obituary columns. She confessed to her *Paris Review* interviewer, in a slightly less facetious moment, that her famous short story "Big Blonde" was probably based on someone she knew. Taking a poke at women writers who worked in a different genre, she said: "To those who write fantasies . . . I am not at home."[1]

Italo Calvino, a writer who was less sociable than his work might suggest, didn't miss the opportunity to joke with his interviewer—who, incidentally, was his beloved translator into

English, William Weaver—by pointing out that he planned all of his books in detail, and that particularly in his tarot book *The Castle of Crossed Destinies*, the most calculated of them all, nothing is left to the cards.

José Saramago also used to say that he would spend months—after a random idea had gripped him—planning a new novel from start to finish. He would only begin writing once the title had already been decided. He admitted that, outside of the predetermined plot, the characters themselves could dictate actions, speech, and small changes. The bulk of it, however, was always decided beforehand. But this wasn't what happened with his most commercially successful book, *Blindness*.

In this case, according to the great Portuguese writer, the characters took control of the plot. As his wife, Pilar del Río, also told me, it was above all the women in the novel who made Saramago completely change the course of the story, something that had never happened before, and to a degree that would never happen again. Let's see what the author recorded in his *Lanzarote Notebooks* while writing *Blindness*:

> After two hours I thought I should stop: The blind people in the story didn't want to go where I wanted them to. Now, when this happens, whether the characters are blind or sighted, the trick is to pretend you've forgotten about them, give them time, let them think they're free,

> so that the next day, off guard, they can be rounded up again, and so on. The character's final freedom is made up of a succession of temporary arrests and freedoms.[2]

When Saramago concluded the book, with his peculiar irony, he stated that "of the initial idea, I'd say that everything and almost nothing remains."[3] The characters, according to Saramago, demanded humanity during the writing of the novel: "It took me far too long to realize that my blind people could do without a name, but they couldn't live without humanity."[4]

If this happens to writers who try to plan their books in detail, we can imagine what happens to others who sit down at their desk with only an inkling, or only a character who appears before the story in which they will become the protagonist. John Cheever claimed to work this way. E. M. Forster is said to have had an even looser point of departure. The author of *A Passage to India* is quoted by Saul Bellow—in the interview he gave *The Paris Review*—as having once said: "How do I know what I think until I see what I say?"[5]

Bellow used Forster's line to explain that, when writing, he would set loose the commentator within him, for whom he had to prepare the ground. Only in this way would the "primitive commentator," who lived in his mind, remember colors, shoes, phrases, or words he might never have seen or heard.

The past thus serves as a shadow for the writer—both the one held in memory and the one personified by the sentence newly written on paper or on a screen, which begs to be continued. Hemingway said, "Sometimes you make it up as you go along," and "Everything changes as it moves."[6] Ricardo Piglia was of the same opinion. In his diaries, he wrote, "How can you know which is the best, among all the possible stories that present themselves while you are writing? It is always about making decisions; writing is making decisions. I never know what the story will be like until I write it. And as I write it, I let myself be led by intuition and the rhythm of the prose."[7]

Years ago, I wrote some fairly amateurish short stories that were somewhat memoiristic in nature. In one, the narrator, a boy, remembers sitting on the dining room floor during the art history classes that his mother used to host for a group of friends. The teacher was missing a leg, which attracted the narrator's attention whenever he peeked under the table and saw an odd number of legs. I had, in fact, attended these classes, sometimes sitting on my mother's lap, sometimes on the floor. In the story, I gazed at the art teacher. From under the table, I heard her strong Italian accent and, staring at her legs, I thought about the missing one. What was the real impact of that scene on my childhood? Was I so impressed by the teacher's missing leg that I needed to fictionalize it? Or did I simply remember it because the image I remembered fit the literary moment, was useful to the story in question, in which I sought to portray the character as a lonely boy, an only child, an odd one out, like the teacher's leg?

Once again, it's an unanswerable question. All I know is that if Descartes had been a writer of fiction instead of a philosopher, one of these phrases might have gone down in history: "I remember, therefore I write" or "I write, therefore I think."

Once again, for any writer, the opening of a book is vital. In his dense and beautiful book *Beginnings*, Edward Said argues that before any beginning, there is always the idea of beginning.[8] The opening of a novel can always be considered a new beginning, the moment when, based on previously acquired ties shared by both reader and author, the narrator's voice and authority are established.

Amos Oz, in *The Story Begins*, explains that the opening passage is a contract that binds author and reader. A contract that can be broken—and often is—during the making of the text or as it is read.

Oz says that the page that will receive the first lines of a book is, for the writer, "actually a whitewashed wall with no door and no window." For him, beginning to tell a story is like "making a pass at a total stranger in a restaurant."[9]

The book about an unhappy editor that I never wrote had some basis in reality. Undoubtedly, a seasoned professional begins evaluating a book from its opening paragraph and, in many cases, is able to intuit whether or not to continue from there. It is true that some beginnings fall far short of the book's full content. Oz cites the case of Dostoevsky's novella "White Nights," whose beginning is banal, sentimental even. So he wonders: Is the fact that the task of beginning a book is so difficult the reason some authors give up halfway through? Is that why they begin their books without a truly meaningful first paragraph? "God knows," he says, "how many drafts upon drafts he made, re-wrote, destroyed, cursed, scribbled, crumpled, threw onto the fire, drowned in the lavatory, before finally settling for this sort of 'so be it.'"[10]

But the matter isn't that simple. According to the Israeli writer, we must be careful: In "White Nights," the first-person narration is from the point of view of a sentimental character, and the simplistic beginning may have been deliberately banal, to establish the narrative tone.

In this sense, the idea of the contract between author and reader holds. Kafka's *Metamorphosis*, for example, demands an immediate understanding with the narrator, allowing us to enter the author's world of fantasy. In Susan Bernofsky's translation, we read:

> When Gregor Samsa woke one morning from troubled dreams, he found himself transformed right there in his bed into some sort of monstrous insect. He was lying on his back—which was hard, like a carapace—and when he raised his head a little he saw his curved brown belly segmented by rigid arches atop which the blanket, already slipping, was just barely managing to cling. His many legs, pitifully thin compared to the rest of him, waved helplessly before his eyes.[11]

This is one of the most emblematic opening passages of all time. In it, the contract will not be broken until the end. The Czech writer is forever inviting us into a world from which we can't escape until the very end. I'm willing to bet that those who have read this fantastic fable took a while to put the book down and return to their daily lives, and that when they did, they were no longer the same.

Each of us carries, etched in memory, the opening passages that have impacted us the most. Oz cites several of his favorites, but he particularly mentions the opening paragraph of Dante's *Divine Comedy*, which he considers the ideal opening for all books, or even the perfect metaphor for the situation in which authors find themselves when beginning to write. "Midway in our life's journey, I went astray / from the straight road and woke to find myself / alone in a dark wood."[12]

While thinking about this chapter, I tried to return to the openings of novels that had most impressed me, and I immediately remembered how Albert Camus begins one of my favorite books of all time: "Maman died today. Or yesterday maybe, I don't know. I got a telegram from the home: 'Mother deceased. Funeral tomorrow. Faithfully yours.' That doesn't mean anything. Maybe it was yesterday."[13]

The contract between the author and readers of *The Stranger* is established here. Furthermore, the contract that the work proposes includes Meursault's indifference to his mother's death, the fact that he did not cry at her funeral, and the constant presence of the sun and heat, which will accompany the narrator through several passages of the book, from the burial to a crime he committed, from the crime to his trial, and from the trial to his incarceration.

Nothing from the past matters, only the present and chance. However, by Amos Oz's reasoning, there will come a point when this contract is broken. We see that the contract proposed by Camus is strictly adhered to throughout much of the book, through the reiterations mentioned above. However, this will change at the end. When he is arrested, Meursault says: "I realized that this cell was my last home, a dead end, so to speak." Afterward, the character lives exclusively in the past, and states that if he had only one day to fill his memories, that one day would be enough. The contract is broken at the end of the book. The past does matter, and he doesn't come out of his mother's death unscathed, as his indifference in the first paragraph or lack of tears at the funeral might suggest.

It really is worth paying attention to the opening passages of books as, for better or for worse, editors do. The brilliant beginning of *Anna Karenina*, Oz reminds us, is also very interesting and well known. Without going into why, he says that throughout the book Tolstoy contradicts the phrase with which he begins his novel: "All happy families resemble one another; every unhappy family is unhappy in its own fashion."[14] This contract, which he calls philosophical, is broken as the book progresses.

I understand Oz to mean that Tolstoy's novel is so rich that it proves that not even in happiness are we all alike. Or even that the sentence could be inverted and begin the same novel with the assertion that we are alike in unhappiness and unique in joy.

I like beginnings that discredit or relativize the narrator's power, as Miguel de Cervantes, Laurence Sterne, and Machado de Assis brilliantly do in *Don Quixote*; *The Life and Opinions of Tristram Shandy, Gentleman*; and *The Posthumous Memoirs of Brás Cubas*. In them, the reader is warned from the outset that the contract being entered into is not the most reliable, or it is signed by an unreliable narrator, from whom we wouldn't even buy a box of matches. It will be broken in the next line, or a few paragraphs later. Besides these novels, perhaps the most memorable beginning of a book for me is Julio Cortázar's *Hopscotch*:

> Would I find La Maga? Most of the time it was just a case of my putting in an appearance, going along the Rue de Seine to the arch leading into the Quai de Conti, and I would see her slender form against the olive-ashen light which floats along the river as she crossed back and forth on the Pont des Arts, or leaned over the iron rail looking at the water. It was quite natural for me to climb the steps to the bridge, go into its narrowness and over to where La Maga stood. She would smile and show no surprise, convinced as she was, the same as I, that casual meetings are apt to be just the opposite, and that people who make dates are the same kind who need lines on their writing paper, or who always squeeze their toothpaste up from the bottom of the tube.[15]

This is how the Argentinean author begins a novel in which he proposes that the reader choose two possible orders in which to follow the chapters. It's almost an explicit invitation to stumble on the story by surprise, without a set time or place, as the narrator Horacio Oliveira and his mysterious friend La Maga did in the streets of Paris and on the banks of the Seine. After all, isn't this kind of chance encounter what we seek when we open a book?

8.

How Far Can We Go?

It's impossible to generalize or create a rule as to how far an editor can go in his or her work. The answer differs from case to case, depending on the original we're working on and our relationship with the author. Some writers are more open to suggestions, while others are not at all; in some cases authors change their attitude toward their editors over time.

The novelist and writer of short stories João Gilberto Noll was very resistant to change, and rightly so. His texts were very tight and possessed a particular logic, difficult for anyone but himself to unpack. Sérgio Sant'Anna changed over time. Toward the end of his life, he began to accept more input. Some of his later short stories were among his best, but that doesn't mean that it was largely due to editorial influence. Many of his earlier stories and classic novellas were published with virtually no input.

The hallowed writer of crime fiction Rubem Fonseca, on the other hand, was happy to take on board editorial suggestions, almost always in their entirety. I have mentioned here only authors who are no longer with us. I can say, however, that the dialogue with the various generations of writers with whom we work is often intense, often resulting in changes to passages or even a book's final format. Even in this case, I never attribute any more significance to the role played by myself or Companhia's editors, as I believe our responsibility is simply to identify things that were already in the text and that, in the avalanche of writing, authors sometimes miss. We step in when it is agreed that an extra pair of eyes is required, the gaze of an author after the book has been written, only this time from someone else's perspective. It's as if we borrow the writer's gaze and then return it.

Carlo Ginzburg, in his book *Clues, Myths, and the Historical Method*, says that a good historian uses a system of evidence, searching, like Sherlock Holmes, for tiny details that will shine a light on the story.[1] The same can be said of editors: We look for details hidden in the text.

Ginzburg begins the range of examples of his evidentiary method with Giovanni Morelli, the great nineteenth-century art historian who specialized in verifying a painting's attribution. Morelli looked for proof in minor details that were often peripheral to the canvases he studied. To this end, for example, he conducted a detailed analysis of the earlobes in Botticelli's paintings. He used to say that the smiles in da Vinci's works were of little use to him, as were the famous eyes raised to the heavens in Perugino's paintings.

The Italian historian also mentions Sigmund Freud, whose theory proposed examining symptoms in order to arrive at a deep understanding of the human soul. The methods of Morelli, Freud, and Conan Doyle's famous detective are analogous to the work of editors, who examine the details to get to the heart of a work of literature.

It is important to note that I never edit a book on my own; I share the task with another editor. In this way, the first reading of a manuscript is part of an effort that will be increasingly collaborative.

We've made suggestions that have led to an author reworking a book for many years. On the other hand, some of our observations are taken on board and resolved in a matter of minutes. The final decision is always theirs. How they choose to respond to our input can result in two years or a few hours of work. We do not participate in any way in the authorship of their books, and even when our suggestions are substantial, our importance should always be kept in perspective. It may seem contradictory, but we are merely the first readers of a text, putting ourselves in the writer's shoes after they have worked by themselves on a book for months or even years. We act as a natural extension of the creator's mind.

At the same time, we think like someone for whom the book is intended. And we ask ourselves how the reader will react to the text. This is a constant question throughout our reading. Two poles, two loyalties.

During the writing of a book, it isn't always easy to be completely clear about what's taking place. In this sense, we act as an author's double, or a generous reincarnation of them after they have finished writing. Therefore, we can never be overbearing in what we say, no matter how necessary it may be. And this power to suggest or intervene shouldn't alter our humility in life or in literature. Any merit belongs entirely to the authors, whose perspective we borrow, anticipating so many other perspectives that will emerge once the book is published.

Is an editor's work important in arriving at the final version of a book? I believe it often is, but it is always an indirect, remote merit that should remain in the shadows. The authorship remains intact; the writer signs the final version of their book, but a qualified first reader can be a big help. He or she locates the original logic of the text and gives it back to the author, with notes in the margins. The place where we make our suggestions reveals the scope of our participation. We've already seen that a page in a book is a symbolic space. Thus, the margin, which will belong to the reader, along with the spaces between lines, is temporarily occupied by the editor.

In contrast, let's look at Milan Kundera's definition of the artistry found in novels—or, by extension, in literature. In *The Art of the Novel* he posits that the novel casts permanent light on the "world of life" and protects it from "the forgetting of being."[2] Furthermore, he says, "the novel knew the unconscious before Freud, the class struggle before Marx, it practiced phenomenology . . . before the phenomenologists."[3] Because it concentrates within itself the wisdom of uncertainty, the novel is the most profound way to know the self in the modern world.

I couldn't agree more with the Czech writer. With this notion of the greatness of literature, we must take the opportunity and ask our fellow editors once again: At the end of the day, what is the scope of our role, and who are we to take credit?

We need to find the legitimacy to work with something so grand and personal, and we do so as representatives of readers, who will be the next on the scene. When the book is ready to be released, we shift to the opposite role. We represent the authors in all their interests, in dealing with the press and the general public. In this way, we adopt the perspective of readers and the writer at different moments in a book's trajectory. So that the two sides that matter in the book's story find a shared fluency.

When we work on a manuscript, a deep relationship develops between us and the author, which in many cases can be compared to a marriage, in all of its complexity. The editor Max Perkins, whom I mentioned earlier, said that Thomas Wolfe was like the son he'd never had—he was father to five daughters. However, their relationship blended Perkins's paternal feelings with certain aspects of a typical couple's relationship. The end of their relationship seems like the story of a son wanting to free himself from his father, or a lover seeking to free himself from a partner on whom he depends. Although Perkins played an important role in the lives and works of F. Scott Fitzgerald and Ernest Hemingway, among many others, nothing compares to the bond he developed with Thomas Wolfe.

It was, to an extent, this story that gave rise to the myth of the American editor as an interventionist who actively participates in the making of books. An oft-cited story is that of Perkins and Wolfe locked themselves in a room every night for months on end, where the writer typed new pages to flesh out parts of his books' plots that Perkins had excised. According to publishing lore, these same pages were tossed on the floor and later retrieved by Perkins to be cut up and reassembled in a different order, with new excisions, thus composing the final text. This is, of course, an extreme example. Few authors are as prolix and chaotic as Wolfe, just as there aren't too many editors with Perkins's talent and dedication.

The reputation of American editors isn't always justified. Nowadays, many editors in the United States and other countries suggest few changes to originals, especially those of established authors, whose literary agents are their privileged interlocutors and first professional readers because they don't want to deal with editors' criticism or requests for rewrites. The agents, in turn, contribute far less than they should, fearing they might offend their clients. As a result, there is now a surplus of famous authors and a shortage of publishers with initiative. Of course, there are exceptions. With my book *The Absent Moon: A Memoir of a Short Childhood and a Long Depression*[4] in the United States, I was fortunate to have an editor, Scott Moyers, who belongs to the Max Perkins school of editing.

In Wolfe's few and epically long books, Perkins, in fact, played a unique role. Working from raw material, and based on the creative chaos of a tumultuous writer, he assembled texts that have left a mark on North American culture. Scott Berg, the editor's biographer, recounts that the originals of Wolfe's works were so long that, on one occasion, Scribner had to go fetch them in a pickup truck.[5] To bring the author's first book, *Look Homeward, Angel*, into the world, Perkins worked for months, cutting and cutting, tidying up the text, asking Wolfe for new bits to give the book cohesion. This resulted in a volume of 1,100 pages. In the case of his second book, whose first version was one million words long, the two worked together in the editor's office six nights a week for months. Perkins saw the "lone wolf"—his nickname for Wolfe—more than he did his own family. The million words in *Of Time and the River* were whittled down to 450,000, and the novel ended up being published almost without the knowledge of Wolfe, who still wanted to refine the text. The writer was right this time, as, in the rush, more than two hundred copyediting and continuity errors slipped past.

In addition to working for years on two immense manuscripts, the Scribner editor took on the responsibility of sorting out his author's emotional and love life, continually encouraging him not to throw everything away. Perkins would follow Wolfe on long drinking binges and bar crawls through New York or whatever city they happened to be in. On two occasions, he had to accompany the "lone wolf" on one of his favorite pastimes: returning to the apartments where he had written his masterpieces, even if accessing them required climbing fire escapes and jumping out of windows. Other people were living in them. In some cases, they ran into trouble.

The love between two people as different as they were complementary inevitably ended in a fight—with a unilateral breakup on Wolfe's part. Before they parted ways, Wolfe dedicated *Of Time and the River* to Perkins, in an affectionate paragraph that the publisher wished he had rejected for two reasons: first, out of modesty, but also because he sensed that the dedication was a sign that Wolfe would soon turn against him. He had already done this with Aline Bernstein, an older woman who had been Wolfe's lover for several years and who had been instrumental in difficult moments of the writer's life.

In such a peculiar relationship, where the publisher's dedication is unlimited and in which he must remain invisible, the potential for problems and future breakups is enormous. Some authors also struggle to accept that an editor, often younger than them—which wasn't the case with Wolfe and Perkins—takes on such a paternal and protective role in their lives.

Deep respect for the author and the reader—as the parties who truly must have a voice in the publishing process—makes modesty an obligation for the editor, not to mention fundamental to his or her work. When an editor can't bear anonymity or lacks the temperament required for the role, things will invariably go wrong. By failing to fulfill their role as intermediary and being unable to control their own ego, the professional in question will lose their publishing house's main asset in a short period of time. They will see their authors depart, seeking a place where the competition is between equals, not between editor and writer. Interestingly, the difficulty is often on the part of the author, as it isn't always easy to accept an editor's devotion. It requires modesty and a spirit of collaboration, precisely in an art that is produced individually in the deepest solitude. This was the case with Wolfe and Perkins. The writer turned against his father, or lover, from whom he could no longer bear to receive so much.

It is interesting to note that Perkins was asked on more than one occasion why he had never considered becoming a writer, after such intense creative work with his authors. The answer came easily and directly:

"Because I'm an editor!"

There aren't too many examples of this, however. Perhaps there haven't been many Perkinses scattered about the publishing world.

There is the famous case of Raymond Carver's short stories, heavily edited by Gordon Lish, at Knopf, during the 1960s and '70s. When the 1981 book *What We Talk About When We Talk About Love* was published, the author rebelled against Lish's many interventions. Because of the style of his work, Carver was considered a leader of the minimalist movement. But this may be due less to Carver's style than to the enormous number of cuts made by his editor. An uncut edition of the book, edited by two University of Hartford professors, William L. Stull and Maureen P. Carroll, was released in 2009 in the United States.[6] Opinions are divided, with many preferring the writer invented by the editor. However, there are ethical questions surrounding the imposition of such profound changes on a book, with or without the author's consent. Carver certainly approved the final text at the time, but later regretted it, publishing a collection of short stories in the version he deemed best in 1988.

In an essay in *Into the Looking-Glass Wood*, Alberto Manguel questions whether the involvement of a professional like Perkins is beneficial to books. Manguel—a writer with whom I usually tend to agree—not only discusses Fitzgerald's editor but also the case of the verses that Ezra Pound, as editor, eliminated from T. S. Eliot's epic poem, *The Waste Land*. Based on the passages suppressed, Manguel claims to prefer Eliot's poem in its original form. In choosing this example and citing, with good reason, the intellectually fragile stance of some contemporary editors, the Argentinean essayist somewhat overlooks the best thing an editor can offer his or her authors: total dedication, from the most meticulous reading to the resolution of problems that are often outside of their writing. It is true that editors with authorial urges can get in the way of books that don't need them.

The arrogance with which many colleagues approach the profession is troubling. Carver's predicament is one such example. But I prefer to look to good editorial work and defend those who know how to exercise their profession fully and sensitively. Nevertheless, it is interesting to hear Manguel's provocative argument, as the history of publishing has seen in all kinds of cases.

The lines Pound cut from Eliot's poem remind me that Eliot, after a brief stint in banking, was invited by Geoffrey Faber to become an editor at what would become Faber & Faber, a position he held for a long time. I don't know any stories about Eliot the editor, except for his famous rejection of George Orwell's *Animal Farm*. At Faber, he was primarily a poetry editor, but he ended up unwittingly playing a fundamental role in ensuring that his publishing house thrived for decades as one of the world's great independent publishers. Faber's future was sealed when Andrew Lloyd Webber, the wizard of Broadway musicals, decided to stage a book of poems about felines written by Eliot, many years after his death, thus creating *Cats*, the hugely successful musical that ran on Broadway for eighteen years. Faber & Faber remained independent in an environment dominated by large corporations, with part of its earnings, until just a few years ago, coming from box office royalties from *Cats*, paid directly to the publisher.

There is also a curious anecdote about this important English publisher. Geoffrey Faber was initially a partner of Sir Maurice and Lady Alsina Gwyer at Faber & Gwyer. With the departure of the Gwyer family, he renamed his label with two Fabers instead of one. According to legend, Geoffrey did this to give the impression he had another partner, whom he could blame for rejecting the manuscripts he decided not to publish.

It strikes me that many author-editor breakups happen because the author's work and the publisher's editorial direction are no longer as compatible as they once were. Also, like in a romantic relationship, an editor whose devotion to an author is almost unconditional will want to continue publishing the author's work, without realizing that his love is no longer the same. He wants to hold on to it, less for the books to come than for what they've already done together. Or out of jealousy at the thought of seeing the author with another publisher, where they may be more successful than he could have made them. It's hard for the editor to recognize that the passion has waned, or that the relationship is more dependent on the past than on the present. This is perhaps one of the reasons why so many breakups are initiated by the author. I'm not referring here to purely commercial breakups, which can be initiated by either party. The separation is painful, but the next day might not be as difficult as the editor imagined. In many cases, literature has already left the couple, and there is no other desire capable of keeping them together forever.

9.

Oliver

Meeting Oliver Sacks was one of the greatest privileges of my professional life. I was a big admirer of his work, and one of his books, *Seeing Voices*—written when we were already friends—inspired me to try writing a novel. Luckily, I abandoned that endeavor in time.

Oliver was captivated by the covers we created for his books, designed by French artist Zaven Paré and the Brazilian graphic artist Hélio de Almeida. They were abstract, with bold colors. It was my idea to have them like that, covered in acetate with the title and his name. The art reproduced the multiplicity of colors that emanated from the great neurologist's work. In it, Sacks talks about the brain and human emotions in a simple yet very literary style. The human mind in his books is like an involuntary romance, full of colors and singularities.

Given that his assistant, Kate Edgar, had said that those covers were among his favorites, I plucked up the courage and invited him to lunch during one of my stays in New York.

It worked. We met at a Japanese restaurant near his office in the Village. He was very quiet, wearing a suit that looked like armor on a man who clearly needed space and wasn't used to that kind of attire. I never saw him dressed so formally ever again. In the middle of lunch, without excusing himself, he left the restaurant to pace down the street. Kate explained that Oliver couldn't stay still in one place for very long. I watched as he walked over to one of those manhole covers typical of New York streets, out of which billow clouds of white steam. He stood there for a few moments, breathing in the vapor that no one else goes near. Intrigued, I watched him in his gray suit, arms behind his back, leaning over the steam. After that, lunch continued to go well; I wasn't shy, and Kate helped a lot. I realized that day that Oliver Sacks had a stutter. When he came to Brazil for the first time, I worried about this fact before his lecture at a theater in Rio de Janeiro. I didn't bring it up, of course, but after the lecture, in which he spoke fluently, he told me that he didn't stutter in public events. In this aspect, Oliver was like a subject in his book *An Anthropologist on Mars*, the surgeon with Tourette's syndrome, who only in the operating room doesn't tremble, lose control, or swear. Sacks was deeply moved by the fact that a woman took it upon herself to translate the event into sign language from a corner of the stage. It was magical.

As I write this text, I wonder how I had the courage to suggest our first meeting, something unusual between a foreign editor and a writer. An author of Oliver Sacks's stature might have around forty editors scattered across the globe. There's no way he could spend time with them all. There would be no time to write. What's more, I can't say how I made the leap from that first meeting to frequent contact, each time I visited New York. Additionally, Oliver was one of the authors who sent me more than one letter, typed on beautiful writing paper, commenting on the editions of his books in Brazil. I created this space with many writers. I wonder if, with my increasing shyness, I would still be capable of the social ease I felt on so many occasions in the past? Indeed, I was a different person. Maybe in a professional capacity, I'd be able to do it again today, but I have my doubts. I've become much more withdrawn and antisocial. On the other hand, it's easy to be like that after a few achievements and with a great team of editors. But my audacity, or chutzpah, might still be the same.

The writer's two visits to Brazil were memorable. He made a couple of requests in order to visit the country: free time for phone sessions with his psychoanalyst, and a pool at least twenty-five meters long for his daily swim. At the Copacabana Palace Hotel, where we hosted him, this last wish was granted. In São Paulo, we made an arrangement with Clube Pinheiros to use their pool. In Rio, Oliver and his traveling companion went for a swim at Prainha, at the end of Barra da Tijuca. A driver hired by Companhia das Letras accompanied them. After a considerable time, the driver began to get worried. He scanned the horizon and couldn't see them. He was beginning to fear the worst when Oliver and his friend appeared. They had swum quite a distance, perhaps even out to the open sea.

While in Rio de Janeiro, his greatest pleasure was visiting the botanical gardens. He spent hours there, examining each plant in detail. This had also been one of his requests: to visit the park created by Dom João VI—the Portuguese king who fled to Brazil and made it the seat of his empire when Napoleon invaded Portugal—which contained specimens that couldn't be found anywhere else.

In São Paulo, the highlight of his visit was a trip downtown with my wife, Lili. There, they visited the Botica ao Veado d'Ouro, an old-fashioned pharmacy with medicinal ingredients, most in powder or liquid form, stored in thick glass apothecary jars. Oliver was moved by what he saw. Afterward, they went to the used bookstore Sebo do Messias, which he also left in awe. If memory serves me, he bought a book of poetry in English. Overall, he loved the old city center.

A lecture was scheduled for the next day in the auditorium of the São Paulo Museum of Art. At dinner the night before, I had taken advantage of the intimacy we'd acquired and asked him how he managed to speak so well to large audiences.

"Luiz, I choose one person in the audience and speak only to them, the whole time."

The night of the conference, I gave a brief presentation of his work and, when I gave him the floor, I took a seat beside him. My mother often attended Companhia das Letras's events, and on this particular occasion, she was sitting in the front row. Suddenly, in the middle of Oliver's speech, I looked over and saw that she was fast asleep, snoring with her head slumped forward. I began to panic: What if she was the one he had chosen to focus on? What's more, at the end of book launches, to my embarrassment, Mirta would often introduce herself to the authors, telling them that she was my mother. That couldn't happen that night! I started shaking my head, grimacing, and moving my hands, but I couldn't leave the stage to go wake her up. I made sure she didn't introduce herself to the author. I made an excuse and pulled her away from the autograph queue.

Our catch-ups in New York brought us closer together. I would go to his office almost every time I was in the city. On one visit, he played the piano. On another, he ordered Japanese food for our lunch. The food came, we ate, and washed the dishes.

On one occasion, there was a brief awkwardness between us. After reading *Seeing Voices*, I fell in love with the story of the feral children who never mastered any more elaborate use of language. They were fashionable in the eighteenth century, when they were locked up and displayed like exotic objects in cages for the royalty, in castles, and, in some cases, for common people. They were a counterpoint to the Enlightenment. In his book, Oliver delves into the stories of Victor of Aveyron and Kaspar Hauser, where there is a struggle between language and nature. Fascinated by this excerpt of *Seeing Voices*, I began researching the real-life stories of Mowgli and Robinson Crusoe. The story of the castaway who inspired Defoe to write his famous book seems to have been very different from the one that appears in the book. Living among animals in the wild, the castaway loses his ability to speak and, once found, takes a while to regain it. The Scottish sailor did not tame nature, as legend has it, but was dominated by it. Mowgli's story also differs greatly from the books and films about him. Taken from the jungle and living among humans, the story of the wolf boy Dina Sanichar, who inspired the fable, definitely does not have a happy ending.

With the doors this book opened for me, I decided to try to write a novel that would include all of these lives and also that of the sculptor Franz Xaver Messerschmidt, a strange artist linked to theories of mesmerism, who created sixty busts with different human expressions, which were astonishingly lifelike.[1] Silence and the difficulty of expressing oneself were favorite topics of mine, so I tried to use parts of Sacks's book as inspiration for a novel. My writing was poor and overly scholarly—I had researched all those cases and had little imagination. That was the last time I attempted a foray into the genre.

In the middle of the process, still enthused with the subject, I went to visit Oliver and started talking nonstop about it, especially the Austrian sculptor. The neurologist interrupted me, putting me in my place:

"I'm not here to hear about your book, Luiz, but to talk about what I'm writing right now."

I realized the enormity of my blunder, and proceeded to give my full attention to the author and the text he was writing. Oliver Sacks often confided in me the topics of his next books.

Once, he told me he suffered from prosopagnosia, a disorder that makes it difficult to recognize human faces. He said he paid attention to voices, height, and the outlines of people's faces so he could function better socially. On another occasion, he told me about the cancer that had caused him to lose sight in one of his eyes. He spoke at length, blending medical knowledge with personal circumstances. Later, this tumor would metastasize to his liver, fierce and surprising. Oliver didn't just write about his problem with sight at the end of his life. In a moving text, he described his feelings about his impending death. He was living happily with a new partner after coming out as gay.

Meeting our idols in person isn't always nice. That wasn't the case with Oliver Sacks. What a privilege it was to know him beyond his books. I went to his memorial service, where Kate Edgar introduced me to his boyfriend. It was wonderful to see the love the writer found late in life. His secretary was tasked with keeping the flame of Sacks's work alive, and has done so very successfully. At the service, I recalled the time I took Oliver out to eat at one of São Paulo's excellent sushi restaurants. As we dined, my mind flashed back to the beginning of our friendship, in New York, when that big man bent over to inhale steam from the street.

10.

Pride and Power

Nothing is more important in an editor's life than the discovery of a new literary talent. This is the moment in which we actively contribute to our country's culture. Just as the suggestions we make when reading a manuscript are secondary to the original itself (since the things we point out are already in the originals, in their logic and conception), so too is our discovery of a young author less important than the merits of the author and the text that was there before we read it. Meanwhile, there are excellent books out there that have been missed or unfairly rejected.

Let's return to the case of Max Perkins, well known in publishing circles. The protagonist of this story was a US army officer, who, afraid he would be deployed overseas, sent "a grab bag of stories, poems, and sketches"[1] to Charles Scribner's traditional and conservative publishing house. Having received only unfavorable in-house readings, the originals reached Perkins, who recognized in them an unpolished talent. The author was Lieutenant F. Scott Fitzgerald, who had now gained a champion for his future as a writer. Perkins wrote him a rejection letter, offering general observations about the problems identified in the work and encouraging him to submit new material. Fitzgerald worked on his text and submitted a revised version weeks later. However, the original was rejected again by the editorial committee. The main difficulty at the time was overcoming the conservatism of Charles Scribner Jr. and other veteran editors, getting them to accept Fitzgerald's modern, colloquial language, which would be even harder a few years later in the case of Hemingway, whom Fitzgerald brought to Scribner.

Perkins was persistent and managed to convince the young man to rework the book once more, according to his instructions. The third time the original was accepted and Perkins sent a jubilant letter to Fitzgerald announcing that *This Side of Paradise* would finally be published.

In the early decades of the twentieth century, in addition to a backward mindset on the part of editors, there was a fear of moral censure from critics and society. Perkins's fabulous story continued as he made the first novel by the young author—who years later would go on to write *The Great Gatsby*—into a huge commercial success. Perkins, says his biographer, "treated literature as a matter of life and death."

I was moved countless times while reading Perkins's biography. I discovered something grand in my profession, a grandness to which I have never come close. But what caught my attention most was learning that the genesis of the great American editor's work was in the struggle for a talent to be recognized, seeking to approve the publication of an innovative young writer in a notoriously traditional and backward environment.

In Brazil's case, we have the figure of Augusto Frederico Schmidt, who published Jorge Amado's first book, *O país do carnaval*.[2] Schmidt also discovered the great Brazilian writer Graciliano Ramos—surprisingly, through reading reports written by Ramos, who was the mayor of a city in the interior of Alagoas. Recognizing the literary quality of those political documents, Schmidt instructed his secretary, Rômulo de Castro, to send letters to the author. "With a text like this, he must have a novel," Schmidt told his assistant. And he did. After some time and much insistence, *Caetés* reached Schmidt, who, months later, distracted, thought he had lost the original. It was meant for posterity, however, because he had actually forgotten it in the pocket of a thick raincoat, and published it not long afterward.

Another important example is that of sociologist Gilberto Freyre, with *The Masters and the Slaves*—also published by

Livraria Schmidt Editora, the small publisher's first commercial success. Schmidt's work as an editor is highly praised, but a combination of dilettantism and pessimistic print runs made the company short-lived. Its beginnings were linked to a group of Catholic intellectuals, most of whom were aligned with the Integralists, a fascist political party. Schmidt's Livraria Católica, which later dropped the *Católica* from its name, initially brought together "Catholics, fascists, and communists."[3] Later, lost in many other pursuits, including his own writing, and with no faith in the potential of the Brazilian market, Schmidt saw his authors migrate to other publishing houses and ended up closing.[4]

At this point, another hero emerged, very different from Perkins or Schmidt, but equally valuable. He was José Olympio Pereira Filho. He began working young, first as a pharmacy clerk and then as an assistant bookseller, dusting and opening boxes at Casa Garraux bookstore. In the future, he would secure funds to purchase two important private book collections and found his own bookstore, largely stocked with foreign titles. Like other houses in the sector, it would become a meeting place for young intellectuals and aspiring writers.

But what would make José Olympio a truly distinctive publisher wasn't, initially, his discovery of writers, a good many of whom had come from another publishing house, but rather his treatment of them. Olympio believed in Brazil and its literature before and much more than most of his contemporaries. It was he who boldly transformed authors into true professionals, with guaranteed advances and large initial print runs. José Lins do Rego is an example of a writer who would move to his new publishing house after being with two others. He migrated, seduced by the financial and professional offers, which he boasted about publicly.

Max Perkins and José Olympio were very different editors—most of the editorial work at the latter was done by José Olympio's brother, Daniel Pereira. What they had in common was their respect for authors. It is this dedication that underpins our profession. Editors who lack this characteristic tend to fail. That's why Perkins and Olympio, each in his own way, did our profession proud.

Another aspect of the author-editor relationship, beyond the positive attributes listed above, is the complex authority wielded by editors. There are stories, not always edifying, of moments both sensitive and problematic. Discovering a writer like F. Scott Fitzgerald or Graciliano Ramos is a momentous thing in an editor's life. The experience of guaranteeing professional status to authors such as José Lins do Rego, Jorge Amado, and Manuel Bandeira is equally fundamental. Nevertheless, editors—whether enjoying moments of importance or not—should always remember that flirting with glory does not become us.

A life filled with professional accolades can often lead to hubris when dealing with the work of others—a form of abuse in the exercise of our so-called power. A typical example is the mistakes we make when rejecting manuscripts without giving them the consideration they deserve, sometimes passing over excellent books based on superficial or arbitrary assessments. Our profession grants us an authority that is often misused.

There are countless legendary cases far less edifying than those at the beginning of this chapter. Editors' rejections and mistakes have become the stuff of publishing folklore and are worth remembering, perhaps the most notorious being the rejection of Marcel Proust's *In Search of Lost Time* by André Gide, then an editor at Gallimard. Gide, who after many years became Proust's friend, confessed to having returned the original manuscript of one of the masterpieces of world literature after reading two or three passages at random. Even after it was accepted by Grasset, an editor of *In Search of Lost Time* asked why "a man should take 30 pages to describe how he turns over in his bed before he goes to sleep."[5]

Another famous case is T. S. Eliot's rejection of George Orwell's *Animal Farm*, which I mentioned earlier. The original, which is a harsh allegorical critique of the Soviet regime and all forms of authoritarianism, was rejected by a number of publishers, including Faber & Faber, where the famous poet worked as a director. It is well known that several of the novel's rejections were motivated by an unwillingness to displease Joseph Stalin—then England's wartime ally. In his letter, T. S. Eliot (negatively) qualifies Orwell's book as Trotskyite. I include excerpts from the letter below:

13 July 1944.

Dear Orwell,

. . . On the other hand, we have no conviction (and I am sure none of the other directors would have) that this is the right point of view from which to criticise the political situation at the present time. . . .

Now I think my own dissatisfaction with this apologue is that the effect is simply one of negation. It ought to excite some sympathy with what the author wants, as well as sympathy with his objections to something: and the positive point of view, which I take to be generally Trotskyite, is not convincing. . . . And after all, your pigs are far more intelligent than the other animals, and therefore the best qualified to run the farm—in fact, there couldn't have been an Animal Farm at all without them: so that what was needed, (someone might argue), was not more communism but more public-spirited pigs. . . .

Yours sincerely,

T. S. Eliot[6]

Jack Kerouac also struggled to get *On the Road* published. Two editors at Knopf, one of North America's best and most pioneering publishing houses, said of the icon of beat literature:

"This is a badly misdirected talent and . . . this huge sprawling and inconclusive novel would probably have small sales and sardonic indignant reviews from every side."

"I don't dig this one at all."[7]

Anne Frank's *The Diary of a Young Girl* was rejected fifteen times, once with the justification that the book lacked feeling or a worldview that might arouse readers' curiosity. The opinion the book received, again from Alfred Knopf's publishing house, called it "very dull" and "a dreary record of typical family bickering, petty annoyances and adolescent emotions. . . . Sales would be small because the main characters were neither familiar to Americans nor especially appealing."[8]

Nabokov's *Lolita* was turned down widely in the United States and had to be published in France by a publisher of erotica, Olympia Press. Legend has it that one of the rejections came with the recommendation that it "be buried under a stone for a thousand years."[9]

An editor said of Herman Melville's *Moby-Dick*: "Does it have to be a whale? . . . Could not the Captain be struggling with a depravity towards young, perhaps voluptuous, maidens?"[10]

Flaubert read from his future editor: "Let us take full charge of the publication of your novel . . . ; we will make the cuts that we think are indispensable. . . . My private opinion is that if you do not do this you will be compromising your entire career. . . . Be brave, close your eyes during the operation. . . . You have buried your novel underneath a heap of details which are well done but utterly superfluous."[11] The author of *Madame Bovary* did not accept the proposal and demanded that his book be published without cuts. The rest of the story is well known.

Stephen King, after sending *Carrie* to several publishers, received a letter that said: "We are not interested in science fiction which deals with negative utopias. They do not sell."[12]

The works of Gertrude Stein and Kurt Vonnegut and the *Harry Potter* series, among many others, languished for years before receiving a favorable opinion from a publisher. One letter addressed to Stein is among the most iconic for its aggressiveness:

Dear Madam,

I am only one, only one, only one. Only one being, one at the same time. Not two, not three, only one. Only one life to live, only sixty minutes in one hour. Only one pair of eyes. Only one brain. Only one being. Being only one, having only one pair of eyes, having only one time, having only one life, I cannot read your M.S. three or four times. Not even one time. Only one look, only one look is enough. Hardly one copy would sell here. Hardly one. Hardly one . . .

Sincerely yours,
A. C. Fifield[13]

Although I am not aware of any letters quite this arrogant written by Brazilian editors, it is common in this country for manuscripts to go unread, due to the enormous difficulty of keeping up with the book proposals submitted. It isn't possible to dedicate the time necessary to everyone who wishes to become a novelist. In the United States and many other countries, manuscripts aren't even read when they're sent by post, but are only reviewed when they come to publishers through literary agents, who represent the authors and act as a filter for those who have a chance of getting published. We have excellent agents, but there aren't many of them, and they could never take on the number of aspiring writers scattered all over Brazil. As such, without professional or personal sponsorship, we no doubt miss out on discovering many talents. There are lucky occasions when we choose a book without a recommendation. It is incredibly satisfying when this happens.

Companhia das Letras has made many mistakes rejecting certain foreign titles. One of them was the *Harry Potter* series, which Liz Calder, the books' English editor, suggested to us before it became the success it did. Lili, who was in charge of young adult books at the time, was working on a postdoctoral degree, so we sent the series to an external reviewer. We rejected it, claiming there were better Brazilian creations. I still can't believe we did that. The works of Elena Ferrante and *A Game of Thrones* were turned down for being too long.

We certainly make mistakes when it comes to Brazilian books, perhaps to a lesser extent. Errors are very common, the result of human failings, but they can also be a prompt for professional questioning. After all, where does an editor's decision-making ability come from? What gives us such power? A knowledge with no origin in science, which depends primarily on one's sensitivity and is based mostly on dedication to the cause of literature? In this case, the instruction booklet for "editorial authority" should come with the recommendation "Use with moderation."

Good professionals can make themselves heard by their authors even on the most delicate issues of textual intervention. Standing side by side with our writers at all times is what makes these interventions possible. By representing them, we essentially seek to fulfill two of a writer's most sincere wishes: to produce the best literary work possible and to reach a large number of readers.

To question my own authority and balance it with effective service to authors is the best way I've found to live with the seductive power that characterizes our professional position. Exercising authority without neglecting human values is a good start. Practicing the profession without being dazzled by it is even better. Tempering my ability to interfere in people's lives with humility, compassion, and self-criticism is what completes my quest for editorial dignity. There are sensitive moments in an editor's work. It is impossible to avoid conflict when rejecting a text or when we need to reconcile the needs of the publisher, authors, and readers. We must edit books without ever losing our tenderness.[14]

11.

James Joyce Meets Adelaide Carraro

Earlier I told the story of how Random House was founded in 1927 by Bennett Cerf and Donald Klopfer. Interestingly, the new publisher's first bestseller wouldn't come along until 1934, and quite unexpectedly—as is often the case with bestsellers. What's more, Random House's biggest sales success was born of a landmark achievement in the defense of freedom of expression.

Excerpts of James Joyce's *Ulysses* were first published in the United States in 1918 in *The Little Review*. The reaction was immediate. With the poet Ezra Pound as literary editor, the periodical, as its name suggests, was small in both circulation and budget. The magazine's problems with censorship had begun in 1917, after the publication of a short story by Wyndham Lewis about a British soldier who gets a woman pregnant during World War I and ignores her calls. The text was considered "obscene" at a time when concerns about espionage and patriotism were intertwined with mores and moral censorship. *Ulysses* was an even bigger problem.[1] At the time, the agency responsible for censorship was the United States Post Office, which had three hundred thousand employees spread throughout the country. With its brutal and widespread power, and in a context of external and internal conflict, its actions were extremely arbitrary. It is said, in fact, that the censors' concern with James Joyce began with his nationality. During World War I, a significant number of Irishmen were working as spies, for they thought that supporting Germany was a way to weaken the United Kingdom and pave the way for their country's independence. Even though Pound had cut some of the more hard-hitting passages, when the first fragments were printed in *The Little Review*, the text was quickly banned (the censorship regime didn't actually notice the text until after the war was over, but it was still in operation), making it impossible to publish the book in its entirety in the United States.

The nation's war interests and people's difficulty distinguishing between anarchism and free speech are important in understanding the mindset of book censors, not only then but generally. Under the Espionage Act, which was enlisted to ban literary works, freedom of expression was literally considered a crime. One of the first censored excerpts of *Ulysses* in *The Little Review* is a reminiscence in which Leopold and Molly's affection merely culminates in passionate kissing. But the situation would continue, ever escalating, with the same magazine attempting to publish new excerpts. The work's successive bans began in the United States in January 1919, and continued for many years, until the famous court ruling of 1933. In England, the legal challenges continued for some time as well. The most daring literature continued to be considered a risk to society, and Joyce was admonished in the streets of Paris, where he was once called an "abominable writer." The "literary anarchism" of a sublime text, which had nothing subversive about it other than its language, had such great charisma that various conservative factions joined forces against it.

With *Ulysses* banned in the United States and England, the only English edition available was put out by the Parisian publishing house and bookstore Shakespeare and Company and occasionally smuggled to other countries by those eager to read the Irish author's masterpiece. Ernest Hemingway is said to have been one of the book's biggest smugglers.

In 1932, Bennett Cerf asked the owner of the Parisian bookstore to arrange a meeting with Joyce, from whom he obtained the North American rights to publish *Ulysses*. Cerf organized a legal battle to end the ban on the work in the United States. He hired the renowned lawyer Morris Ernst, offering him a share of the book's royalties if the ban was lifted. The lawyer, who would end up receiving royalties until *Ulysses* entered the public domain—a victory that made him a millionaire—prepared his defense by putting together a special edition of the book, consisting of just one copy. This volume included the most important published reviews of the text, by renowned authors such as Ezra Pound, Edmund Wilson, and Ford Madox Ford. The next step was to have that copy brought to the United States and seized at customs. Only then could a legal challenge be brought against the ban.

To ensure that it was seized, Cerf sent an agent to await the traveler bringing in the special volume, which had been deliberately battered to make it look like a worn copy of the work. The agent then reported the traveler to customs officials, saying he knew he was smuggling a prohibited item into the country. The customs officers weren't interested in the offense, and the agent had to loudly demand that the traveler's luggage be inspected. When they opened his suitcase, they once again refused to seize the book, claiming that everyone arriving from Paris had a copy of *Ulysses* with them. It took a great deal of insistence, and more shouting, for the item to be confiscated. That was the moment at which a legal challenge became possible. Ernst defended the book brilliantly, in what would become a famous manifesto for creative freedom, concluding, "If this book is to be banned, then literature is a ghost and our culture is a prison. But if this book is to be free, then the mind itself is free." In 1934, two years after Cerf's first contact with Joyce, *Ulysses* was finally published in the United States.

With the previous ban and the legal campaign for artistic freedom as pillars of the book's publicity campaign, one of the most difficult novels in the English language became a huge bestseller—the young publisher's first and, until then, biggest.

In *At Random*,[2] Cerf also recounts a later battle he fought for Joyce's *Ulysses*. To promote the book in as many outlets as possible, the publisher approached the American News Company, which had a large distribution network spread across the country. Cerf's jubilation at selling five thousand copies of such a difficult work in outlets intended for purely commercial products may seem prosaic to a publisher working today. But what Cerf achieved for the type of book in question, at a time when print runs and average sales were much lower, was an extraordinary feat.

I fully understand Cerf's joy on that occasion. Victory became jurisprudence for freedom of speech, and was followed by the commercial success of a masterpiece: Could there be a more meaningful example for those who fought or who continue to fight to popularize complex works of world literature and older forms of art?

Many years later, another, even more serious case of banning was that of Salman Rushdie's *The Satanic Verses*, when an order to assassinate the author was issued by the Ayatollah Ruhollah Khomeini to all Muslims on February 14, 1989.

The proclamation began with the phrase "We are from Allah and to Allah we shall return!" The ruling was extended to the work's translators and editors. The writer went into hiding, protected by Scotland Yard. His Japanese translator was attacked and stabbed to death. His Italian translator was also stabbed, but survived. The Norwegian editor was shot and wounded. Salman remained in hiding for a long time, but returned to public life many years ago, assuming the fatwa had been forgotten. On August 12, 2022, a young man named Hadi Matar, after some online research, decided to carry out the thirty-three-year-old order. He followed the writer to the Chautauqua Institution in upstate New York, where Salman was to give a lecture. There, taking advantage of the lack of special security, he rushed onto the stage and stabbed Salman twelve times. After a long period in the hospital and several surgeries, Salman survived, but lost movement in one hand and his sight in one eye. It was a very close brush with death, at a time when he imagined he was free to live a normal life. I wrote to him while he was in the hospital and cried when he later replied, "Luiz, I am on my way back."

What happened to *The Satanic Verses* in Brazil is also worthy of note. When the work was published in English, Salman's Brazilian publisher was Guanabara, whose literary list was led by Pedro Paulo de Senna Madureira. Before the fatwa, Andrew Wylie, Salman's literary agent, wanted to relocate him to a different Brazilian publisher. He spoke to me during the Frankfurt Book Fair and agreed to send me Salman's new book. Shortly after our conversation, I went on vacation with my family. The hotel where we were staying had only one TV, which was in a room next to the lobby. One night, watching the evening news, I learned of the terrifying attack on the writer. I immediately called my secretary and asked if any unopened packages had arrived from the Wylie, Aitken & Stone agency. At the time, books were sent in print copies. On top of the pile was an envelope containing *The Satanic Verses*. I asked her to keep the package sealed and not to mention it to anyone.

When I returned from my trip, there was already a buzz about the book's fate in Brazil. I asked for two expert opinions on the work: one from Rubem Fonseca, who was openly in favor of publishing it, and another from Paulo Francis, who was against it. The magazine *Veja* called me asking if I was going to publish the novel. I said I was waiting on the readers' opinions. I had already decided to publish *The Satanic Verses*, but I needed to buy time. The journalist's response was "You're mad, you're Jewish!" I said I didn't care, that it was my duty to fight a decree such as that one, but that I was waiting for the readers' opinions.

A short time later, Alfredo Machado, of Editora Record, announced that he would be willing to publish the work as a symbolic act of freedom of speech. I spoke with my partner and employees, and to my surprise, a senior member of Companhia was vehemently opposed to the publication. The argument was that we'd be putting the physical safety of many people at risk. I had no choice but to accept the objection. When I communicated the decision, with great discomfort, *Veja* published an article criticizing the cowardice of Brazilian publishers. Alfredo Machado backpedaled, saying that my refusal had brought the book bad publicity and that, as a result, it wouldn't sell. He attempted to form a consortium of five publishers to bring it out. I argued that we should extend it to any publisher willing to speak out in favor of freedom of speech, and I approached professional organizations. Both the Brazilian Book Chamber and the National Union of Book Publishers were opposed to the undertaking. I spoke with Fernando Morais, then secretary of culture for the state of São Paulo, who agreed to lead the consortium. I breathed a sigh of relief, but only briefly. The governor vetoed the joint publication through the State Department of Culture.

A few years later, I managed to overcome resistance within Companhia and published *The Satanic Verses*. The writer was living with some freedom, still protected by Scotland Yard, but he accepted my invitation to come to Brazil. Before him, we received an emissary from the British secret service, who came to scrutinize every detail of the visit. We were told that Scotland Yard could only operate on British territory, so Rushdie's stay in the country would be supervised by the Brazilian Federal Police. It was at this point that the trip began to become unfeasible. During his stay, the writer would have to wear a bulletproof vest and wouldn't be able to circulate in public places, even to attend a soccer match. In hindsight, perhaps they were right. In the meantime, I believe that a publicist who knew about the visit, because he worked for us, told a society column about Salman's arrival. The matter was extremely confidential, for obvious reasons. The columnist published a note saying something to the effect of "If you got on a flight and the author of *The Satanic Verses* was sitting next to you, what would you do? Well, it's about to happen. Salman Rushdie is coming to Brazil."

Following this statement, the Federal Police stepped up its demands. Companhia das Letras had to close off two entire floors of the hotel where the writer was to stay and pay for them. It also had to hire two armored cars and pay the officers assigned to the task. Naturally, we had to abort the trip, informing Salman that if he came to Brazil, he'd be held hostage by the Federal Police, trapped in a security system even stricter than Scotland Yard's. Besides, we could never cover all the proposed expenses.

Later, Salman would come to the country three times, in complete freedom. Neither he nor we could have imagined that the curse cast on him by the ayatollah would come back to haunt him so many years later.

These days, banning books is back in vogue in the United States. Across the country, conservative groups and parents have filed lawsuits demanding that books be removed from public and school libraries. "Moral activists" who serve on school boards and in school districts have successfully banned from their libraries works by Harper Lee, Margaret Atwood, Anne Frank, Aldous Huxley, John Steinbeck, Mark Twain, John Green, and Dav Pilkey (author of *Captain Underpants*), among so many others. The list is enormous. At the time of this writing, it affected 1,207 authors, 268 illustrators, and 14 translators. The state with the highest number of bans, by far, is Florida, whose laws permit this practice. Most of the censored works are aimed at young audiences, and a good number of them feature Black characters. The racial bias expressed in book censorship is glaring. It comes disguised as a moral complaint. Among the banned writers are world literary luminaries such as Toni Morrison and Alice Walker.

The practice is widespread across most US states. Some institutions are fighting the upsurge in censorship, but the truth is that nearly 80 percent of cases go unnoticed. Recently, Penguin Random House courageously filed a legal challenge together with the Iowa State Education Association to fight a state law that allows book bans. A school, a student, two teachers, a librarian, and four authors, including John Green and Jodi Picoult, joined the challenge. Under this new Iowa law, books containing descriptions or illustrations of anything erotic, or about gender identity and sexual orientation, are banned in public and school libraries. The publisher and its partners are trying to demonstrate that there should be freedom to portray everything in literature without classifying important works of young adult and world literature as pornography. They are seeking to defend citizens' rights through federal law, which guarantees freedom of speech. The Iowa state law, which gave rise to a lawsuit from the world's largest publisher, is paradoxical—a sixteen-year-old can have sex and watch erotic material online, yet they can't read about it. A significant portion of the banned books, it should be noted, does not have sexual content as a central part of the narrative. Penguin Random House has also launched a campaign called Let Kids Read as a further step toward ending this discriminatory practice. These actions honor the memory of the publisher's founder, Bennett Cerf.

More recently, the five biggest publishers in the United States, led by Penguin Random House, filed a new lawsuit, this time against an Idaho state law that allows, among other acts of censorship, parents of minors to request the banning of literary works they deem inappropriate for young people to read. Additionally, in the early days of the Trump administration's second term, threats were made to military schools if they did not act on book bans, as in the previous examples. In the state of Tennessee, more than 1,400 books were removed from public school libraries from 2023 to the end of 2024. Like works on the subjects mentioned above, books such as *Vive la France*, about the French Resistance during World War II; *A Game of Thrones*; and Andrew Solomon's classic *Far from the Tree*, about various types of parenting, were banned.

Unfortunately, in recent years there have been frequent attempts to ban books for moral reasons in Brazil. The numbers are lower than in the United States, but the cases are serious. The outcry and push to ban books in private schools comes from parents, who want to prevent works containing violence or any mention of sex from reaching their children, even when they are already in high school. But there are also public censorship initiatives, spearheaded by congressmen and aldermen from various parts of the country.

For example, there have been instances of book banning in the southern state of Santa Catarina, where Bolsonaro's influence has been strong in recent times. There, the state government banned from all schools books such as *A Clockwork Orange* by Anthony Burgess, *It* by Stephen King, *The Chemistry Between Us* by Larry Young and Brian Alexander, along with nine other titles. In this case, the censors' fear had more to do with the genres of horror and dystopian literature. Recently, a conservative congressman demanded that Marçal Aquino's book *I'd Receive the Worst News from Your Beautiful Lips* be struck from the entrance exam for the University of Rio Verde, in Goiás. Writer Luisa Geisler was uninvited from a book festival in Nova Hartz, Rio Grande do Sul, by the local government. The reasons for these acts of censorship aren't always clear; they are usually arbitrary and have their origins in the radical far-right group that has taken over part of the country.

Writer Jeferson Tenório and his important book *The Dark Side of Skin* have been the target of censorship. The novel, which won the Jabuti Prize, shows, via a well-spun plot, the practice of racism in Brazil. In 2022, Jeferson accepted an invitation to participate in a debate with students from the Land

School in Salvador, which had adopted the book in classrooms. Before leaving for the Bahian capital, the writer began to receive death threats on his Instagram account through an anonymous profile. The event went ahead, but it had to be held online, as the school could not guarantee the author's physical safety. In 2024, the same work, which had been selected in 2022 for an important Ministry of Education program, was attacked online by a school principal and subsequently removed from schools by the regional department of education. When this was met with widespread outrage, the institution backed down. The incident occurred in the city of Santa Cruz do Sul, Rio Grande do Sul. The alleged reason was the presence of "profanities" in the novel. The purchase of books under the National Textbook Program (PNLD) is decentralized and subject to the scrutiny of teachers and education specialists. The principal who protested had signed the purchase form for *The Dark Side of Skin* for her school. This is yet another instance in which racism parades as the defense of morality and decency. While in this case the veto was lifted, the principal's video resonated with pro-Bolsonaro groups, and requests to recall the book were subsequently issued in the states of Paraná, Goiás, and Mato Grosso do Sul. Through our lawyers, we managed to have the federal government's decision to purchase the books upheld and the books returned to libraries in two states: Paraná and Goiás. Like in the

United States, what is implicit in these acts of censorship is, in addition to political motivation, a failure to understand the maturity of young readers over the age of fifteen, and the moralistic abuse of power, challenging the educational standards of impeccable professionals hired by the publishers and the Ministry of Education. Behind it all lies hidden racism, calling a book that denounces police violence against Black people a pornographic novel.

Going back in history, during Brazil's military dictatorship, the censors banned around 220 books, both fiction and nonfiction. Interestingly, the same banning for moral reasons was already very present back then, causing authors of erotic pulp fiction like Cassandra Rios, Adelaide Carraro, and others to become the most-banned authors in military Brazil. Lumping these cases of censorship and banning in the same basket with more literary books and other genres is interesting. What could James Joyce and Cassandra Rios possibly have in common? Both cases demonstrate the absurd moral excuse that underlies most censorship decisions from ultraconservative groups.

Important works of Brazilian literature, such as *Feliz Ano Novo* (Happy New Year) by Rubem Fonseca, *Zero* by Ignácio de Loyola Brandão, and *The Wedding* by Nelson Rodrigues, as well as books by historians Caio Prado Jr. and Darcy Ribeiro and Brazil's former president Fernando Henrique Cardoso, all received the label "banned." The same went for dozens of plays by Plínio Marcos and Oduvaldo Vianna Filho, among so many others.

It's true that book censorship during the Years of Lead wasn't terribly effective. It may have inhibited new editions, but in practice, the government machinery wasn't able to remove books from circulation. Censorship wasn't prior to release, as it was with newspapers, which were few in number and where censors could work in loco. How could one control in advance the approximately ten thousand titles published annually by the country's hundreds of publishers? Although some works by political scientists were banned from circulation, many others, by the very same authors or other analysts of the military regime, made it into bookstores. With writing of the highest quality, they tore apart the Brazil of the dictatorship. Editors were true heroes and demonstrated the importance of working against authoritarianism through literature, essays, and works that denounced the dictatorship. Notable among them were Ênio Silveira at Civilização Brasileira, Jorge Zahar at Zahar, Fernando Gasparian at Paz e Terra and the magazine *Argumento*, and Caio Graco Prado at Brasiliense.

All these sorry stories serve as a reminder of how wonderful it is to be able to choose what we want to read. If a book offends a reader morally, all they have to do is dismiss it, so that those who don't share the same opinion can enjoy it freely. This way, young people will be treated as mature individuals, capable of exercising choice. In the case of young readers, the choice of books falls to teachers and parents, who must also have the freedom to do so. Without freedom, we can't live to our fullest.

12.

José

Saramago was sitting in the middle of the room, reading aloud from a typed page with some handwritten corrections on it. That meant he was in the final stage of writing a new book, ready to type up a final copy of the whole text, without any mistakes, and send it to his Portuguese publisher. Before this phase, he had thought about the original for approximately six months without writing anything, then he had handwritten a first draft. Only afterward did he type the text twice—one version for corrections, the other not.

I listened to him read, mouth agape, unable to believe I was alone in that apartment with José and his wife, Pilar. He was reading me a passage from *The History of the Siege of Lisbon*—his first book to be released simultaneously in Portugal and Brazil. It was the second of his works to be published by Companhia das Letras. The first was *The Stone Raft*, which we released some while after the Portuguese edition.

At the time, José and Pilar lived in a charming apartment on Rua dos Ferreiros à Estrela, in Lisbon. I was staying at York House Hotel, on Rua das Janelas Verdes. The street names—literally "street of blacksmiths that leads to (the neighborhood of) Estrela" and "street of green windows"—felt like something straight out of José Saramago's books.

Pilar had arranged everything for that trip of mine, during which she took me to some of the places that were settings in *The Year of the Death of Ricardo Reis*. At the end of my stay in Lisbon, the Spanish journalist—who hadn't been with the writer for very long—asked me to accompany her to the Amoreiras Shopping Center, where she was going to buy José his first computer, which we ended up choosing together. The typewritten work I had seen in his hands was to be the last. For future manuscripts, a word processor would take over.

I had met the couple in person a short time before that, when they had come to Brazil for the launch of *The Stone Raft*. José's work was more popular in Rio de Janeiro, where the tour began. The humorist and playwright Millôr Fernandes had discovered *Baltasar and Blimunda* and talked it up all over the city. Lili and I went to Rio for that first encounter, and we all stayed at the same hotel—the one I always stayed at—the Ouro Verde, in Copacabana.

We all hit it off immediately, with a trip to the beach and strolls along the seashore arm in arm. There's a photo of José Saramago in swimming trunks, gazing at the horizon.

I stupidly ended up abusing that closeness and made a tasteless joke. Brazilians often joke about the Portuguese, but that time I crossed the line. I asked José if it was true that the Alfred Hitchcock films *Vertigo* and *Psycho* had been released in Portugal with spoilers in their titles, as *The Woman Who Lived Twice* and *The Father Who Was the Mother*, respectively. He, quite rightly, didn't find it funny at all and vehemently denied it. He was generous enough not to call off the beginning of our professional relationship and friendship. Not even my young age could justify such foolishness on my part.

From then on, everything went very well, and we grew closer and closer. Encouraged by the harmony of our budding friendship, José made a request before leaving Brazil. "I'd rather not stay in hotels anymore when I come to São Paulo. I'd like to stay at your house, with Pilar." José had a deep aversion to hotels, where he would spend an increasing amount of time as his international career took off. So, for several years, our daughter Júlia would be temporarily moved to her brother Pedro's room so

José and Pilar could stay in hers. When we moved to a larger house, they stayed in the room reserved for our granddaughters' visits.

This is how the deepest connection I've ever had with a foreign writer developed. Pilar played a fundamental role, becoming practically a member of the family. And it had all begun by chance.

Because that is how I acquired the rights to José Saramago's work—after casually telling his agent in my last meeting at the 1987 Frankfurt Book Fair that I had read *Baltasar and Blimunda* and considered it one of my all-time favorite books.

Ray-Güde Mertin was startled and asked if I had a specific reason for saying that. Then she asked me to stop by the fair again before heading to the airport. José's work was about to be transferred to another Brazilian publisher at that very event, but she preferred the young Companhia das Letras. I left my suitcase in the taxi, returned to the venue, and settled all the details for what would become much more than the publication of José's future works—but also an immeasurable friendship. We spent time together at home with each new book or lecture he was invited to give. We discovered José's personal tastes and culinary quirks—like, for example, the fact that he detested coconut. Lili, who loved it, teased him, saying she would write a thesis on the dialectics of coconut.

Two of the writer's birthdays were celebrated at our house, complete with cake, decorations, candles, and all the trimmings.

We traveled to towns in Minas Gerais with the whole family. The Portuguese author hadn't yet won the Nobel Prize, but he was already being stopped in the streets or in the churches we visited. He was always moved by the affection of the Brazilian public.

Once, we went to our countryside retreat in the Mantiqueira Mountains. I gave myself a difficult task. My father, a Holocaust survivor, had been deeply upset by a recent statement by José, after a visit to Ramallah with a group of other writers, in which he had compared Palestine to Auschwitz. I arranged with Lili that we would climb Pedra do Baú—a large, trunk-shaped rock formation—taking the easy path, and that she would leave me alone with José there. Sitting on Bauzinho, the lower of the two peaks, with the vast valley at our feet, I said what needed to be said. I told him my father had called me in tears and that, although I found Israeli expansionism and the treatment of Palestinians unacceptable, I didn't think that the comparison was appropriate at that time. José's reaction was harsh, but over time it softened. Later, he told me that his statement had been distorted by the journalist.

One of our most iconic trips happened when the writer won the Camões Prize. We all went to Brasília, where the award was to be presented by President Fernando Henrique Cardoso. Among the guests were the legendary author Jorge Amado and his wife, Zélia Gattai, also a novelist. José and Pilar had been invited to go to Salvador after the ceremony to stay at Jorge and Zélia's house. Upon receiving the invitation, they asked for it to be extended to Lili and me.

It turned out that the Bahian writer's house had been overrun by termites. As a result, he booked us a hotel in the same neighborhood, Rio Vermelho, just two houses away from where singer-songwriter Caetano Veloso and film producer Paula Lavigne stayed when they were in town. Later, the charming hotel would be bought and turned into singer Gal Costa's home. Jorge organized lunches, at a different house or restaurant each day, choosing places with the best cooks in Salvador. The first lunch was at Caetano's house—a Bahian feijoada made by the composer's brother, a master in culinary arts. It was the day of the Festa da Entrega, when boatmen leave the beach in Rio Vermelho to take offerings to the Candomblé orixá Iemanjá. From the top of Caetano and Paula's house, you could see the celebration. The lunch went from three in the afternoon until three in the morning.

José hadn't brought casual clothes—no shorts or T-shirts. In that intense heat, he ended up wearing mine. That afternoon, José boldly went over to Jorge Amado and told him he should change publishers. I was mortified. Jorge looked at me awkwardly, his eyes saying he couldn't—or didn't want to—make such a move. I responded silently, with just a look to show that I understood the novelist's reaction. José's prediction eventually came true years after Jorge Amado's death.

For part of the evening, José's and Lili organized the manuscript of Caetano Veloso's memoir into several secure files and made copies of everything. The way it was stored, he risked losing everything he had written up to that point.

At every lunch, Jorge Amado's clan of friends joined us. Among them were the artists Calasans Neto and Carybé. During a visit to Carybé's studio, we secretly bought a painting for José and Pilar, and they also bought one as a gift for us. At the end of the visit, we exchanged surprises. Carybé's wife asked us to temporarily loan them the watercolors for an exhibition in Seville, the city where Pilar del Río had spent much of her life. We agreed—and never got the paintings back! They ended up becoming symbolic gifts.

A few days after the first feijoada, there was a traditional concert celebrating the anniversary of the town of Santo Amaro da Purificação. Caetano invited us to the house where he had lived in his hometown, and then to his show, in which his mother, Dona Canô, sat on the stage facing the audience, receiving heartfelt tributes. Everyone who attended the celebration received a button that read "I saw Caetano in Santo Amaro." In the middle of the crowd, José's was approached with requests to autograph the souvenir.

On the return flight from Salvador, José stared out the window at the immensity of the city of São Paulo before turning to us and announcing, "I've just had an idea for a new book." As always, he imagined a book for the first time and gave it a title: *All the Names*, my favorite book by José Saramago.

Lili and I visited the couple's home on the island of Lanzarote after they decided to move there, prompted by an act of censorship in Portugal. It was moving to see José's new workspace, with his records and desk surrounded by dogs. Mozart's operas were his favorite CDs to accompany his writing. We took walks through the stunning volcanic landscape. It felt as if those stones carried the power of the future Nobel laureate's writing. They seemed to leave their silence to enter the pages of his novels. As we walked around the island, José's hair was tossed by the strong wind of the Canary Islands. This image was made immortal in a photograph taken by the acclaimed Brazilian photographer Sebastião Salgado.

One of the most moving moments of our relationship was the announcement and ceremony of the Nobel Prize. How I celebrated in Frankfurt when I heard the news!

José was about to board a flight to Madrid when an airline attendant told him he had won the prize. He returned to the

Frankfurt Book Fair—where he had been promoting some of his books published in Germany—to celebrate the honor with his editors and friends in the publishing industry. Soon after, we prepared for the Nobel ceremony: I rented a tailcoat, and Lili bought a long gown for the occasion. In Stockholm, we spent hours in the couple's presidential suite, where Pilar tried on her beautiful red dress to show Lili. There were two suites of that size and grandeur. In the other one, next door, Bruce Springsteen was staying. José had no idea who he was. At the event, Pilar looked so stunning that the next day, she—not José—appeared on the front page of the main local newspaper.

José entered the palace deeply composed and delivered a masterful speech. The photos are proof: that was not a moment for smiles on his part. Seated at tables with his other editors, we experienced it all with great joy.

Long before the Nobel, shortly after the publication of *The Stone Raft*, José's book signings began to draw crowds of readers. I recall one of his first visits to Rio de Janeiro, at a signing event at Timbre bookstore, where the line wrapped around the escalator. I asked him to only sign the books, without dedications, but he insisted on writing each reader's name before his autograph. In the middle of the event, a woman took Candomblé bead necklaces from her own neck and placed them around José's as a gift or blessing. She hugged and kissed him in reverence. When she was done, José moved and startled, pulled me aside and said, "Luiz, these people are going to kill me with love."

Every time he came to Brazil, the events grew larger. In São Paulo, they began to be held at the SESC cultural center, often opening with readings from his work by renowned actors, actresses, and writers. José refused to limit the number of autographs he gave, so we would often return home in the early hours of the morning. In a tribute to Companhia das Letras, he decided to launch *The Elephant's Journey* first in Brazil, then in Portugal. In my opinion, it was his best book in many years. José arrived in Brazil looking very thin and weak. The lung disease that would eventually take his life had already begun. We arranged lunches at Antiquarius, a top Portuguese restaurant in Rio de Janeiro, with the writers Rubem Fonseca, Ana Miranda, and Chico Buarque, or at home with his longtime friends Leyla Perrone-Moisés, Raduan Nassar, and Lygia Fagundes Telles.

In Rio, this time we stayed at the Copacabana Palace, where a hilarious scene unfolded. José was walking arm in arm with Pilar near the pool, heading toward me. His pace was slow. A socialite who lived in the building next to the hotel and treated the pool as an extension of her home approached me and said, "Who is that? I know him! He's . . . he's . . ." and then ran toward the Portuguese writer shouting, "This is insaaane, it's

García Márquez, this is insaaane, Garcíííía Márquez!" We burst out laughing and didn't correct her. As a result, the socialite, who greeted José Saramago thinking he was his friend Gabo, probably still believes she met the author of *One Hundred Years of Solitude*.

Dmitri Medvedev, then prime minister of Russia, was scheduled to meet President Lula at the hotel, and I, hotheaded as I am, ended up in a kerfuffle with one of Medvedev's bodyguards, who shoved me to make room for a piece of luggage he was carrying. José didn't notice anything, but Lili saved me from a ridiculous fight. It would have been another embarrassment, typical of my temperament, at such an important moment for the writer and for me.

Though increasingly weakened by his illness, José decided he had the strength to write one last book: *Cain*. After that, he felt a renewed urge to create more texts and began *Alabardas, alabardas, espingardas, espingardas* (Halberds, halberds, rifles, rifles), about the global arms industry, which he never finished.

His health deteriorated, and the doctors weren't able to eradicate his lung infection. And so, a few months after José had begun his manifesto against the arms industry, Pilar called me and asked me to open the camera in Skype. She showed me José, dead, lying in his bed. His passing was expected, but seeing him like that was very hard. I prefer to hold on to other images of him—on the beach in Rio, with his oversized glasses, unnoticed by the bathers; signing an autograph at Nossa Senhora do Rosário dos Pretos church in Tiradentes, when he was still amazed at his success in Brazil; or the four of us sitting together, looking over the little garden of his home in Lanzarote.

13.

The Writer Onstage

Flaubert's famous phrase ("I am Madame Bovary") and Fernando Pessoa's renowned verses ("The poet is a faker / Who's so good at his act / He even fakes the pain / Of pain he feels in fact")[1] are oft-cited defenses of literature as pretense. Dostoevsky, the author who wrote with precision about the somber depths of the human soul and nevertheless claimed to believe that "beauty saves the world,"[2] was also a great ideologue of the falseness implicit in literature: "Lying is man's only privilege over all other organisms."[3] The remarkable Russian writer brought these vital matters into some of his novels through his characters.

Fiction, faking or exaggeration, lies or self-deception—literature uses a series of elements that in real life are looked down upon or seen as moral flaws. While in life we seek our own identity, in literature we flee it. While in life we must be honest and modest, in literature exaggeration and deceit are often worth as much as, or more than, reliability.

The best example that occurs to me of a writer who uses exaggeration as a primary resource is the Austrian Thomas Bernhard. His literature is born of rage; it allows no restraint. Often, distortion suits him best—even in the middle of realistic prose. In his wonderful collection of memoirs, *Gathering Evidence*, the author presents himself as immoderate from the outset. He tells us that at the age of eight he climbed for the first time onto a bicycle that belonged to his guardian, and without ever having learned to ride or asking permission, he tried to go alone to Salzburg, thirty kilometers away. The theft of his stepfather's bicycle and his implausible flight to a distant place the very day he learned to ride are essential, marking the beginning of a life of transgressions, in which the narrator is socially displaced at all times. In his novels, some of which are autobiographical, Bernhard is alienated from the world. His exaggerated self, central to his plots, finds a counterpoint in the tedious reality of Austria. A few pages after taking off, having arrived at a friend's house, the author begins to describe what might actually be his first act as a storyteller. He describes himself telling a third party about the feat of the bicycle theft in the following terms:

> I gave him a thoroughly dramatic account, which I was convinced could only be regarded as a highly polished work of art, although it was undoubtedly based on real events and facts. I dwelt a little longer on the points that struck me as most favorable, reinforcing one aspect, attenuating another, always with the climax of the story in view, without preempting any part of the buildup and, moreover, without losing sight of my central role in that dramatic poem of mine.[4]

Further along in the same series of books, Bernhard characterizes himself as a troublemaker: "Everything I write, everything I do is a source of trouble and irritation."[5] And he continues:

> We have contented ourselves with wishing to write and describe the truth, as well as to tell the truth, even though we know that the truth can never be told. The truth which we know is, from the point of view of logic, a lie, and this lie, since we cannot circumvent it, is the truth. . . . In all the years we have spent reading, we have never encountered a single truth, even if again and again what we have read has been factual. Again and again it was lies in the form of truth and truth in the form of lies, etc.[6]

Always choosing life paths that differ vastly from societal expectations, the Austrian writer is a fugitive, and takes the opportunity to characterize human beings, in particular writers and artists, as performers. In another passage, he writes: "A child is always a theater manager, and I was a theater manager from a very young age. . . . We started out from the theater, in the truest sense of the word. Nature is the true theater. And the human beings in this true theater are the actors, from whom nothing much is to be expected any longer."[7]

But while for Bernhard both life and fiction require freedom and pretending, the latter is only successful if it creates a coherent distortion, or theater, from beginning to end. In addition to performing or pretending, distortion is a good definition of what writers most commonly do. However, it should only be present at the base or in the structure of a book. Once the reader has made the leap to the imagined situation, a second deformation comes across as sinful, incoherent, or contradictory. Once the author has entered the fantasy, all he or she need do is keep going, fully presenting what they imagined, until the end of the novel. Forge with conviction; pretend with aplomb; part ways with reality.

It is the editor's job to assess every detail of this fabrication, or, in more colloquial terms, to see if the lie holds water. In truth, we are inspectors of the make-believe, which, let it be said, isn't always an easy task. In our professional lives, we don't discuss whether fictional narratives, and even some memoirs, are based on real events, but rather whether the fiction is able to sustain itself to the end. José Saramago employed a curious kind of distortion in his novels. He would take the literal nature of Portuguese culture and language usage to such a point that the mundane became absurd. He was an absurdist who subverted the way we think in Portuguese. To understand him, one must embark on this radical journey with the language.

What is curious is that reality often seems even more implausible than fiction. As Dostoevsky once stated, "The truth is always implausible."[8]

One of the most frequent accusations leveled at writers is that they are constantly seeking attention. Many believe that authors have delusions of grandeur and have become so accustomed to pretending and acting that in real life they exaggerate even when buying bread at the bakery. Unfortunately, such things do occur—luckily, they are an absolute minority. Even so, I disagree with this assessment. It isn't hard to imagine that, when creating entirely new worlds, fiction writers may sometimes find it hard to move between imagination and reality. And in many cases, that's a good thing.

There are hilarious stories of writers who were great performers and starred in scenes worthy of the best fiction, scenes suited to their screenplays, plays, and novels without any need for revision or copyediting. They did it naturally, without compromising their literary work. Everyday phrases leave or have left their mouths already edited, as if intended for characters, to go straight into the pages of their books. Hemingway, for example, made part of his life a performance, and many of his lines seemed ready-made epigraphs for his books. The playwright Nelson Rodrigues, from Rio de Janeiro, was another who clearly created an extreme and amusing persona for himself. Nowadays, however, uninterrupted performance can be dangerous in a writer's life. We live in times when publishers demand that authors be the main promoters of their works and require that they engage in media performance on a large scale. This performance, in a world dominated by social media, must ring "true"; it can't come across as mere acting. Currently, in the United States, a writer who doesn't have a "platform" from which to talk about his or her work may not even be published by a respected publisher. If an author is averse to interviews, even worse. With media presence playing such an important role in the life of a book, constant performance can be dangerous, as readers often want to meet the writer and are wary of an alter ego that isn't very credible. If this false naturalness of today's world is difficult for most of us, what about those who make a living creating parallel realities? To round it all off, in addition to social media and newspapers, today a writer must take the stage at literary festivals and perform without losing their spontaneity. The character onstage is the writer.

The example of Jonathan Franzen at the tenth edition of the Paraty International Literary Festival is interesting. He had come to launch his novel *Freedom* and was the most anticipated author at the festival. Already poised and ready to speak, he listened to the moderator's introduction and, at a certain point, took a deep breath, looked at the large audience, stood, and began his talk. He was interrupted by Ángel Gurría-Quintana, who said, "Wait, I haven't finished my presentation yet." That moment when the moderator cut off the writer was all it took to remind him that he was in a theater in front of more than five hundred people, having to perform. It was dramatic. The mask slipped, and instead of a polished persona, the audience witnessed a fragile fellow human baring his soul, a real person instead of a writer presenting his work, seeking the audience's approval. Many people felt great empathy for him, realizing they were witnessing a unique moment of the artist as a human being. Perhaps they realized the inherent contradiction of performance in publishing and the difficulty that results from the constant demand for authors to perform. Others didn't see it that way. They certainly didn't expect to see the writer being so nakedly human in public. They wanted a performance.

If writing is by nature performative, as Thomas Bernhard has shown us, an author's public performance doesn't stop there. The publishing system today relies on the author/actor and the actor/marketing professional. As a result, some writers perform themselves so much that they forget about others, the raw material central to their books. Their work withers. Or they stop writing altogether and only attend festivals, in a nearly endless merry-go-round.

However, there are a few cases of authors whose writing is exclusively navel-gazing in nature. The books in this category include many autofiction novels that don't take off, either because they don't speak to a broader context or because they don't delve deeply enough into the author's personal journey to generate any kind of empathy in their readers. This genre should not be confused with the work of Thomas Bernhard that I mentioned above. He looks outside himself, albeit with profound contempt, but he looks. On the other hand, not all books in the genre are deserving of this criticism. There are masterpieces among them.

To this end, we might ask how much of the exhibitionism is the writer's own, if it is a vice inherent to the profession of "social dramaturge," or if it is above all a new marketing practice on the part of publishing houses, intensified by the appearance of literary festivals.

Leaving the pressure exerted on writers by their publishers out of the discussion, we must understand the feelings of those who make a living creating parallel worlds, manipulating entire lives, giving birth, making their characters suffer, climax, kill. When the task of writing is done, how does a writer return to daily life? Away from their desk, do they quickly divest from their characters and go back to looking after themselves, interacting with those around them—dog, doorman, neighbor, family?

Returning to the beginning of this chapter, I'd like to offer another example of how omnipotence resides in the soul of literature. Its essence is born of writers' disingenuousness. And it isn't always a negative thing. On the contrary, it gives the writing greatness.

One of the best novels I have ever read is *Life and Fate* by Vasily Grossman.[9] It offers a broad panorama of Russia during World War II, a portrait of Stalinism, as well as of Nazism. More than this, *Life and Fate* is a moving work of fiction about the proximity of death in the streets of several Russian cities and in the extermination camps run by both regimes. Nothing that can be said about this work is enough. The range of characters and settings, the richness of the descriptions, the author's purity of spirit—everything is bigger in this novel, leading one to wonder if, outside of writing and art, human beings can experience moments as sublime as those afforded by reading this novel. It is one of those books that makes you believe in literature and in humanity.

I mention Vasily Grossman's book to show how, in a work as singular as this one, we find examples of the greatness of fiction and the baring of the writer's soul. Even with such a large cast of characters, at several points Grossman's literature talks about itself, presents its resources and its claws, and demonstrates how the gravitational center of literature is always itself. Deep down, a good writer always pays reverence to his or her craft, explicitly or not. The following examples are taken from *Life and Fate*.

Viktorov, one of the novel's many characters, is a fighter pilot who finds himself walking in a forest. He remembers a book he read long ago, in which a woman is given in marriage to a powerful man she barely knows. Soon after the arranged marriage, the husband is arrested and taken to a wooden tower. The wife, instead of running away to live a free life, now exercising her own choice, sets out to find him. She manages to discover his whereabouts and takes up residence at the foot of the tower, until she learns that he is no longer there. From then on, she kneels before every passerby, begging for information about her companion's fate. After a time, she discovers that the man has been dismembered. She embarks on a long walk to a convent, where she takes a vow of chastity. From this day on, she dedicates her life to religion, but is reluctant to give up her wedding band.

A fable of love, completely displaced from the plot and belonging to another book, is narrated in a rare moment of calm, in a forest clearing during the war—a moment in which a story of a completely different nature occupies a narrative marked by the death of millions of civilians and soldiers. This fable has several uses for Grossman, among which is to remind us that we are on the stage of literature; it is literature that commands the action.

Writers often speak of themselves through their many characters, freeing their dreams from their mind, as Faulkner said. But in literature there is a gravitational, egocentric force that is always asserting itself: Here I am, look how beautiful and powerful I am, I can take you wherever I wish, from a Russian forest in the 1940s to a wooden tower in a previous century, supposedly the product of another writer's imagination, where a great love has been left unfulfilled.

Writers may be exhibitionists by nature, but the nature of their art is even more so. In this brief passage, we can see how the practice of writing leads, albeit covertly, to a kind of display of the writer's resources and ever-surpassable limits. From the same book, I shall take another small example to try to show how literary devices allow the manipulation of authors' real lives.

Many pages after the ones mentioned above, the narrator,

when talking about the scientist Viktor Shtrum, who is at the center of the book's plot, is constantly being tested by Stalin's censors. Grossman concludes: "He hadn't been able to think during the long walk home—not even about his tears on the staircase or his abruptly terminated conversation with Chepyzhin, . . . or about the letter from his mother in the side-pocket of his jacket."[10] The letter in the scientist's jacket pocket takes its inspiration from a crucial aspect of Grossman's own biography. Irineu Franco Perpetuo tells us, in his excellent preface to the Brazilian edition,[11] that it is a fictionalization of the farewell letter Grossman would have liked to have received from his mother, which never happened. The writer had practically abandoned his mother in another city. Grossman had listened to his wife's wishes, leaving his mother to live alone during the war. He probably regretted it deeply. If the author himself had been the character in *Life and Fate* instead of Shtrum and carried that letter in his jacket, he'd never have forgotten her. We ourselves, after reading *Life and Fate*, will never be able to forget her. It is clear here how clever literature can be, how infinite its resources for manipulating reality.

Grossman says that Shtrum wasn't able to think, but he tries to show what he might or should have been thinking. He inverts reality with the letter. By ignoring the letter, Shtrum takes the blame for what Grossman did to his mother. In this manner, the writer finds company for his own weakness in his characters. He makes us think in Shtrum's stead and his own—both are exhausted after so many ordeals.

The Russian writer didn't live to see his book published. In it, the main character—a scientist persecuted by the Soviet regime—received the letter Grossman's mother never sent him. He is thus able to forget about her for a brief moment. The writer—who never received a letter in real life—could never have forgotten. For this reason, he constantly reminds us of its existence, while plunging Shtrum into the despair and exhaustion he himself no doubt also experienced.

Like Grossman and all good writers, we are transported, without realizing it, to the center of the world of fiction, where we become characters, acting and thinking for them, according to the narrator's wishes.

The game of fiction is complex. It has symbolic ebbs and flows that not even the author can explain. How does one combine the depths of literary production with the promotional requirements that a writer faces when the work of writing is done? What sacrifices are made when a work of fiction ends and the author is called into a public sphere of self-promotion whose demands sometimes even clash with what he or she has written?

Today's writers are simultaneously thrust into different realms: intimate and public. In this way, when their imagination needs to materialize in a performance and take to stages more real than those they have invented, we should ask ourselves: What price must be paid in order to promote a book?

14.

The Look of a Book and the Role of Paper

One of the most pleasurable stages of my work is seeing a book take on its physical appearance. In the past, this moment used to come at the very end of the editing process, when the text had been edited and was ready to be published. For the sales and marketing departments, this meant a rush, as the book needed a cover in order to be publicized and put on sale. I remember the days when we would show book covers to bookstores and the press in printed samples, racing to get orders in. In a way, this process made sense. The publisher could only visualize what the book would look like after all the stages of editing were complete, after getting to know the text intimately. Those were different times.

As I started having more contact with foreign publishers, especially those who began to acquire the international rights to Brazilian books, I saw that in other countries books were given a visual identity much earlier. Sometimes almost as soon as an editor had acquired the rights to a work, they had to provide their art department with the information that had led them to take a gamble on the book. A first draft of the cover would be created and everyone in the company would spend time with it before publication. Nowadays, in almost every publishing house, one can walk into an editor's or marketing professional's office and see a less polished print of the cover of a book that is still a long way from being published.

With the digitalization of the entire production process, glossy paper proofs are almost nonexistent and digital art is being created further and further in advance. Visible on our screens, the design comes to life while the text is still being edited or translated by its author or translator. The final version of the artwork may undergo modifications, but it begins to emerge parallel to the editing process.

This discussion has implications beyond those related to practical aspects of the publishing schedule. When we stop to think about the influence of the order in which things are created, we must also consider how the literary nature of the original blends with marketing.

The look of a book isn't born exclusively of its text. Could it indirectly come to bear on the editing process? How to accommodate the cover design while balancing the demands of the book's content and the publisher's business needs?

Common sense provides the answers to such questions. A book is not merely a subjective, artisanal, or artistic product; it is simultaneously part of a commercial network involving publishers, bookstores, and consumers. As such, the question that remains is: How can publishers be respectful of all these unique elements of a book in a market where competition for exposure and success is increasingly fierce? Furthermore, design isn't just about creative or aesthetic decisions. Ethics are involved, as with everything in our daily lives.

The highly anticipated cover largely responds to today's new sales reality, where preorders may be placed months before the publication and have become essential. This is a world in which future or virtual purchases are an irrevocable reality.

Every day, we acquire products that don't yet exist in a material form. In a publisher's day-to-day life, imagining a book that has yet to be written or finished is something we do all the time. We have to take a gamble on originals of which only a few pages have been written, or not even that, based solely on a plan containing the author's proposal. Developing its visual identity well in advance is just another symptom of our times.

But what should a book look like? In an ideal world, especially for works of fiction, it should be neutral enough to allow each reader to create the image of the text they have read in their mind's eye. A very well-defined visual identity that leaves no room for the imagination is disrespectful to readers. Further to my question in the chapter "Whose Book Is This?," I now ask: Where are the "between the lines" of book covers, the space for the reader's imagination?

In literary works, the fewer fixed or figurative images the cover has, predetermining the characters' faces, the greater the space given to the reader's imagination. In the early days of Companhia das Letras, I went as far as to ban covers on which characters' faces appeared with clarity and precision. By placing a well-defined face on the cover of a work of literature, we are imposing our vision of the character on readers.

Over time, with the growth in the number of books published and the fierce competition for space on counters and online bookstores, I have had to relax this principle of mine and can no longer practice what I advocate for above. Even publishers like Gallimard, in France, which used to publish all its books with identical typographic covers, have started using ribbons or dust jackets with illustrations to catch readers' eyes. I confess that even today, publishing more than one book a day across a wide range of genres, I find it strange when a cover looks at me instead of me looking at it.

Narrative fiction still maintains many characteristics of artisanal production. Highly individualized due to their deeply artistic nature, they forge their own path in the mind of each reader. However, they require an industrial system to distribute them in a world where there are more books seeking readers than readers seeking books.

When I was young, I studied and idolized the theorists of the Frankfurt School, who criticized the reproducibility of works of art. Much has changed since then.

I know I contribute to the massification of books, and I take comfort—when anxiety about my role in the publishing world assails me—from the thought that, in this manner, reading in Brazil can become less and less concentrated among the privileged. I don't mean to apologize for changing what I've always done, or for forgetting principles I still admire. In my day-to-day life, most of my decisions are literary or commercial. But politics are also an important element that can come to bear on an editor's choices. Whenever possible, I try to combine all three factors and am much happier when I consider the first and third.

The sociologist Gilberto Vasconcellos, with whom I worked at the Getulio Vargas business school, scornfully remarked a few years ago that the young people who used to read Frankfurt School books with him were now in positions of leadership in the cultural industry. Although I wasn't his student, I had a lot of contact with him at university, and I know that his criticism was partly directed at me. Today, I accept the rules of the market and understand that a masterpiece by James Baldwin or Guimarães Rosa will compete for space in bookstores with purely commercial products. Discreet covers, unfortunately, feel the brunt of the competition.

For example, a few years ago, in our edition of Orhan Pamuk's novel *Snow*, the cover featured a woman staring at the reader with one eye wide open on the front and the other on the back. I was reluctant to accept it, because her features were strong. However, the book was a huge bestseller, and the cover helped. These days, I might waste less time on such a matter. I accept the change, while I'm not always proud of it.

The right cover is the one that most closely mirrors the soul of the book, the one that allows the text's charisma to shine through and capture the interest of readers. If the designer respects this charisma, they will allow the author to speak for him- or herself. They will create a cover that functions as an extension of what is written.

The American composer Aaron Copland, in an interview, refusing to accept the fact that classical music had become a mass product, said that listening to a recording on a record player was like going to bed with a portrait.

It no longer makes sense to discuss the legitimacy of literature's transformation into a product. But perhaps we can still hope that each reader will go to bed with not only a portrait on the cover of their book, but another in their mind's eye.

Having discussed so many topics related to publishing, let us now examine the role of paper in the publication of physical books, given that we've also had digital books for some time now, the kind we see on our tablets when we press the on button, and which vanish on their own when we go to sleep. Several aspects of the paper used in a publication go unnoticed by many readers, but they are no less important. In the global market, physical book sales have been growing, while digital books, after a sharp acceleration in their early days, are beginning to chart a countermovement. Despite this, harbingers of the apocalypse remain on standby. The end of the book as we know it has been foretold since the advent of radio, of television, of digital books, of the internet, of audiobooks, and now of AI.

What explains this long permanence and even the current growth of the book as it was invented in the fifteenth century? Physical contact may be one factor. And, if so, why is it better for so many readers to read on pages that aren't as stark as the very white ones of yesteryear, or on the screens of tablets and iPhones? Why does touching more porous paper with your fingers create a different reading sensation?

After having used cream paper for a long time, we launched a book with completely white paper in order to better show the colors of the black and orange illustrations. When I received the first copy, I confess I was shocked. I wanted to send back the entire print run and change the paper.

From our second year in business, we have increasingly used cream-colored paper developed by a manufacturer for Companhia das Letras. At the time, I was already bothered by Brazilian editions, all printed on conventional offset paper, where the words vibrate more due to the contrast between the dark ink and the very white page. This wasn't the case in other countries, where hardcover editions have long been printed on paper that isn't quite as white, and paperback editions use print that is more refined and grayer in color.

We know that the lower contrast between paper and ink is easier on the eyes while reading. Screens, in this sense, are even worse than the whiteness of some types of paper. They're also not recommended for insomniacs. The iPad turns off with the touch of a finger. The mind doesn't.

In my opinion, that's not all that happens. By marking the completely white pages with black ink during printing, it feels like we're performing a more definitive act. It conveys the feeling that what's printed this way will forever remain as the truth.

In this way, black on white makes the writer's ideas or creativity feel more authoritative. The stark contrast between paper and ink almost seems to make the book into a statement, which, in my opinion, is far from ideal. To believe that a published work won't undergo an intimate elaboration inside the reader is more than just a misconception. It is disrespectful to the reader.

Therefore, paper that is closer in color to the ink, which reduces the contrast between what is said and what is read, ensures greater equality between writer and reader.

Following the same line of reasoning, I believe that porous paper, which is less smooth and uniform, serves an important purpose. When we touch a page before turning it, feeling its irregularities on our skin, we unconsciously connect with something that can change during reading and are reminded that the book has imperfections that make it more human.

In the past, a book had to be opened by the reader using a page cutter. The pages had to be separated one by one, as they came grouped together in "signatures," signaling a task that fell to the reader, not the author, editor, or printer. Each page thus had a different dimension, all created by the imperfection of handmade cuts. And the reader had a role in shaping the final form of the product.

The book, viewed from the side, was not uniform; the individual pages had their own sizes, symbolizing the unforeseen journey of the reader's imagination. The text appeared to physically change in the intervals marked by the alternating pages.

Sometimes it takes us days to return to a book, and everything that seemed established on the page has changed due to our own new state. The unfolding of a novel sometimes accompanies dramatic events in our lives. We might begin a story married and end it alone, or having said goodbye to someone important to us. Is the turning of the page different only because of the new meaning added by the author, the continuation of the story? To this day, some North American publishers have book pages with irregular edges, resembling the editions that used to require readers to open them. I think books that remind us of that time, books that physically mark the differences that will gradually emerge with reading, are wonderful. Additionally, the paper used in their editions is much more porous than that available in Brazil.

I don't mean to say that books were intentionally irregular to signal what I imagine is inherent to the act of reading, but rather that it is possible to attribute these meanings to the material form of a book, since symbols do not come into existence by one's will or intention, but by the spontaneous richness of our inner and social lives.

15.

The Wait

While an editor can sometimes tell if a book is good from the opening passage alone, another challenge for a professional in the field is assessing whether a text ends well. This difficulty, naturally, is greater with fiction than with essays, due to the degree of subjectivity surrounding literary works. It is easier to determine if a work of nonfiction has covered every aspect of a book's core subject. In a novel or collection of short stories, this assessment is always more nebulous.

We know that a novel can begin without much of a bang and grow as it progresses, but at the end readers should feel the book lingering in their minds, even after they have closed it. Curiously, this is a big issue for many writers, especially less experienced ones, who sometimes try to free themselves of a book prematurely.

The task of writing a novel is exhausting. It demands that authors spend a lot of time in their own company, with all of their ghosts, traumas, and repressions. These will no doubt appear on the screen or the blank page. All this mental effort of creation, coupled with the frequent anguish of having time pass without anything productive happening, makes writing psychologically grueling. A seemingly empty workday may not seem terribly trying, but it is very much so. We know, of course, that a productive day results in less fatigue than an unproductive one. Additionally, there are few professions in which there is virtually no one to share one's effort with before reaching the end.

The vast majority of authors say that, after hours of trying to transport themselves into their characters' skin on a daily basis, they feel exhausted, as if they had done a colossal amount of work.

Every writer has his or her own method. Some type on a keyboard or write by hand, initially just allowing their stream of consciousness to flow. Others, however, only want to see the polished text, even in the draft. They write a few lines a day and revise them hundreds of times. And they wear themselves out in this manner, not least because they are holding so many incomplete sentences in their minds for so long. If you have ever been plagued for days on end by a thought or feeling of anguish, you will understand the feeling that assails authors.

In the case of writers who let their thoughts flow onto the screen, they may feel less fatigued, as those full pages signal that the day has been productive. But when it comes time to revise, the exhaustion increases exponentially. Revising what has been poured onto the page is no small task.

Some attribute the phrase "To write is to cut and cut" to Ernest Hemingway. I've heard it said that Carlos Drummond de Andrade, the great Brazilian poet, coined it. It may not have been either of them, but the American writer was a typical example of those who write freely, only to later seek a text's final form. For those who enjoy his short stories more than his novels, therein lies the explanation. Papa, as he was called, appreciated cutting and knew how to do it, which, as we will see, is an absolutely fundamental gift for a good short story writer.

In any case, in the movement of literature, as in all art, there is a striving for perfect expression, with the peculiarity that a writer's work matures at a particularly slow pace. The feeling of exhaustion is also strong because sometimes intuition doesn't mean much to an author. Unless it is followed by a long period of development and a deep dive into the human soul and language, the resulting portrait of the characters will be shallow. A near-perfect sentence isn't found instantly, on the first try. If, in real life, the same thing can be said over and over again, imagine the difficulty of giving voice to a character created from scratch, a being whose reactions depend on the writer or the direction of the plot and who must communicate in a unique way, otherwise they don't belong in the world of literature.

For this reason, most young writers and editors have heard from their first publisher the catchphrase that writing is 95 percent perspiration and only 5 percent inspiration. Caio Graco, my former boss, told me this countless times. Although I consider it something of an exaggeration, I still repeat it to this day.

If we understand the kind of time and effort that goes into writing a novel, it is easier to understand an author's tendency to want to exit it as soon as possible. A seasoned editor can sense when this is about to happen, even before they have finished reading the text. After years and years of reading, I can sense a writer's fatigue before they get to the end. I've lost count of the times I've suggested changes to the final pages of a work of fiction. The writer leaves signs of exhaustion along the way, such as less polished passages that tend to culminate in a hasty ending. In fiction, creator and creation often clash.

As such, novels that overshoot their natural end point are much rarer than those that end before they should.

To my mind, the big difference between short stories and novels lies here—in the shape of a work of fiction and the issue of when to end it. Short stories need to end sooner than expected; a good story will hardly survive if it reaches its conclusion. When this happens, it can become a fable and lose some of its momentum. Generalizations in literature are dangerous, but in most cases, the best short stories are the ones that are open-ended, that almost delegate the ending to the reader. In this sense, if all fiction establishes a partnership between author and reader, in short stories, this partnership comes to fruition in what is left unsaid. Short story writers deliver less; brevity is their challenge. Their silence starts sooner so that the reader's imagination can take over from what would completely wrap things up. Wondering is the main legacy that a short story writer can leave his or her readers.

The writer Rubem Fonseca believed that it was much harder to write short stories than to dedicate oneself to a long narrative. I'm not sure I agree. Each genre presents its own difficulties. The short story demands a supreme effort of condensation and seeks perfection in what is left unsaid, while the novel strives for a kind of comprehensiveness or plenitude. As such, when editing short stories, we sometimes end up focusing more on texts that end later than they should. With novels, on the contrary, it is more common to see cases in which writers have tried to free themselves from a text they can no longer live with.

Sometimes we say that a novel isn't finished or well resolved, meaning that it has ended too soon, that the writer has left rough patches instead of silences along the way. It's as if they haven't fully offered their companionship to the reader. This isn't to say that silence and the unspoken have no place in good novels, but that a good novel manages these things as the text progresses; otherwise there would be no room for the reader's imagination. The wondering that the writer delegates to the reader should not be confused with rushing, which isn't good in any literary genre. A novel crafted over a long period of time allows for a coexistence that shouldn't be interrupted abruptly, while many short stories can use this device very powerfully.

Just as in an earlier chapter I referred to the opening line of *Anna Karenina*—which could be inverted and still make sense—everything I've said here about short stories and novels may make no sense to readers of this book, who might prefer unfinished novels and fable-like short stories whose plots are perfectly stitched up. These are merely my own impressions, dear reader, gathered over a lifetime, which I record here without any insistence.

Since we've already discussed beginnings and endings here, let us now consider the body of a literary text. Many writers come up with convoluted narratives to hook in readers. They seek to win over their audience with unexpected plot twists, which ultimately respond more to the aspirations of the writer's ego—they think they're clever for conceiving so many unusual fantasies—than to the reader's imagination. Trying to seduce the audience with poorly crafted surprises or too many novelties is a common mistake. Some authors may not understand that the most important thing is to create a situation of equality with the reader, a true partnership in which neither side is superior. A rabbit up one's sleeve is a resource for a professional magician, not a fiction writer. It excludes the reader from what has been created in partnership.

There are many books that require surprises, but they must have a solid base, no matter how spectacular they attempt to be. They are part of the plot and don't come out of nowhere. Most of the time, the surprise stands solidly on what has been built along the way, not the opposite. This is the only way it can serve its purpose. Otherwise, the previously mentioned contract between author and reader is broken somewhere in the middle or at the end of the book. Writing is not just a form of artistic display, but an act of surrender that includes generosity and understanding at every step.

There are artists who become arrogant, acting like prima donnas. If this isn't acceptable in private life, why should it be in writing? I would go as far as to say that those who write without generosity, without seeking to place themselves in a position of equality with those at the other end, will hardly create anything of significant literary worth. Even the most cantankerous of writers, such as Thomas Bernhard or Louis-Ferdinand Céline, who repeatedly show a so-called contempt for humanity when they write, do so with respect for their readers. It's as if with their books they were saying: *I despise the world and everyone in it, except for you, the person who is reading my work*. Authors who disparage their readers in their writing are either creating a persona that ultimately speaks to the reader, or they lose sight of the reader.

What holds our attention in a text is the writer's invitation, the suggestion that we wait together at many moments in the plot. In life, we have less and less time for waiting. In literature, waiting is fundamental, and its purpose is more concrete. The writer grants us the opportunity to suspend time, and within this suspension creates other suspensions, which I shall call the wait. When we read, we wait for a detective-style surprise, or take a dive into the psychology of the human mind, or indulge in a saccharine romance, or we allow the author to present us with a unique voice that we don't hear in everyday life. In successful fiction, we come into contact with human fragility. And for that, we need time.

Waiting over and over is what a good piece of fiction offers us. The wait can last a few pages or linger forever in our imagination. This is one of literature's fundamental values, making it even more special in a time in which we tend not to wait for anything. Bad news or tragedies come without warning. Hatred on social media involves no suspension of time. In this sense, waiting in today's world is a political act, implying a certain kind of optimism and belief in the best. And what does good literature offer us if not a wait?

Where am I going with all this? I cannot cover this topic in all its vastness. Nor do I have the expertise of literary critics and psychoanalysts. My goal is much smaller, that of a simple editor.

What makes the content of a book attractive, in my opinion, is precisely how the writer manipulates the various windows that are created during and after the reading. In return, the reader offers the author a place in his or her memory where the writer's creativity will be made eternal. The wait perpetuates itself like a memory, and the relationship between writer and reader will not come undone as long as the narrator's voice is remembered.

Middlesex by Jeffrey Eugenides is a good example of how a novel is crafted. At the beginning of the book, which tells the story of a hermaphrodite, we learn how it ends: that the narrator ends up choosing to assume a male identity. As we read, we are drawn in by the originality of the narrative voice, by the past of the Greek immigrant family living in the United States, by the richness of the many lives that lead us to our protagonist-guide, and, of course, to the character's journey until he comes to be called Cal.

In *Middlesex* the end appears at the beginning, but what counts is the middle. What is fundamental is no longer the book's beginning or ending, but the many other revelations the author administers and offers throughout the story. To secure readers' interest, the writer constantly keeps them waiting, and to this end, he travels back and forth in time, opening up topics that remain inconclusive while introducing other voices and lives. With each window opened during the narrative, a question remains in readers' minds, and even if we don't remember that the topic is there, pending conclusion, the fiction writer captivates and guides us as we follow other stories, until he decides to return to what he left behind.

Another good example is the *My Struggle* series by Norwegian author Karl Ove Knausgård. In this six-novel series, Knausgård transforms his utterly ordinary life into an almost suspenseful narrative, manipulating time and the reader's eagerness. At the beginning of the fourth volume, titled *Dancing in the Dark*,[1] we learn that the subject of the book is the narrator's quest for sexual initiation at the age of eighteen. Knausgård tells us of his move to the Norwegian countryside and his first professional position, as a teacher at a small school in a town near the beautiful Nordic fjords.

The narrative follows his journey to a small village where nothing happens, but which he goes to in search of something vital to him. In the very first pages, we learn that before embarking on this journey the young man has said goodbye to a girlfriend and a female friend, the latter even more affectionate with him than his girlfriend. On the bus, the narrator sees a beautiful girl who looks at him curiously. This attitude raises several questions that will remain with the reader. What will happen to the two "loves" he has left behind? What will become of that exchange of glances on the bus ride? The events that unfold throughout the book are neither numerous nor unique. But the writer creates and manipulates small waits, and perhaps even he cannot predict where they will lead, or how intense they will be. They may even be abandoned. He uses them to simultaneously captivate his readers and guide them through his narrative.

There is a passage in this book that seems emblematic to my argument. I shall end the chapter with it:

> What was this all about? Why did we live like this? Were we waiting for something? In which case, how did we manage to be so patient? For nothing ever happened! Nothing happened! It was always the same! Day

in, day out! Wind and rain, sleet and snow, sun and storm, we did the same. We heard something on the grapevine, went there, came back, sat in his bedroom, heard something else, went by bus, bike, on foot, sat in someone's bedroom. In the summer, we went swimming. That was it.

What was it all about?

We were friends, there was no more than that.

And the waiting, that was life.[2]

Writing a book that includes memories, even if only partially, implies a certain vanity, which is why I've never felt entirely comfortable with the task. I believe that people who achieve some measure of success tend to exaggerate their accomplishments, overlooking two factors that are just as important—or even more so: the influence of chance and of others in our lives. As a way of honoring those to whom I owe so much, I decided to recall our shared history, making clear how vital the richness of companionship and the generosity of others have been to me.

Here, I've combined everything I've thought about my profession and all my experiences with so many authors; from these things, I tried to make a book.

From what I've said in these chapters, it's easy to see how deeply I value the allusive nature of books, how much I consider them living things—the product of a joint creation that sets readers beside the original creators in the most equal way possible.

I read books as every reader does, in a personal and unique way, just as I turn the page trying to absorb as much as I can from it, caressing the paper, even if only for a fleeting moment, before saying goodbye to it and moving on to what awaits me next.

ACKNOWLEDGMENTS

As can be seen in this book's dedication, I owe Lili much more than just her encouragement and understanding during the writing of *The First Reader*. Without her affectionate and loving support at all times, where would my stability and joy in life be?

Lili is joined by my children, Júlia and Pedro, and my granddaughters, Zizi and Alice, in this regard, bringing me such great happiness and making me immensely proud. I thank them for being who they are. The treasures that life has given me. Lais Myrrha and Luiz Henrique Ligabue are part of our family life and provide important support for all of us.

Mirta, my mother, has showered me with affection from the day I was born. I thank her for everything she has given me and for the luminous relationship we maintain.

Otávio Marques da Costa was a friendly and extremely professional editor. He saved the book from taking a wrong turn. He did what I expect of a good editor.

Lucila Lombardi, Márcia Copola, Érico Assis, and Lara Salgado made this book so much better that they deserve every credit imaginable.

Alice Sant'Anna and Ricardo Teperman read the originals and offered invaluable suggestions.

Matinas Suzuki Jr., Mariana Figueiredo, Renata Moritz, Sérgio Rodrigues, and Juliana Leite generously read the first drafts and provided me with invaluable encouragement during moments of self-doubt, which are so common for me.

Good friends like Drauzio Varella and Andrew Solomon have meant a lot to me in my brief writing career. Their words are another guarantee that mine will reach the page.

Eduardo Giannetti and Pérsio Arida complained that my previous book, *The Absent Moon: A Memoir of a Short Childhood and a Long Depression*, didn't touch on my professional life. They planted a seed for this book.

Eliane Trombini is my guardian angel in everyday life. Without her, I wouldn't have the peace of mind to write my books.

Of my eight dogs, Edgar and Bandi were the ones who most closely accompanied a good portion of the sentences I wrote. One in São Paulo and the other in the Mantiqueira Mountains, they lay beside me, dozing to the sound of my computer keyboard and the music I listen to whenever I write. What serenity they gave me as I decided what to say.

To all of my colleagues and authors, I repeat the dedication of this book; without you, nothing I have written would make any sense.

NOTES

INTRODUCTION: THE LAST AND THE FIRST

1. Ricardo Piglia, *O último leitor*, trans. Heloisa Jahn (Companhia das Letras, 2006).

CHAPTER 1: THE BOOK OF CHANCE

1. These and other facts in this text were taken from Charles McGrath's excellent introductory essay to *Alfred A. Knopf, 1915–2015: A Century of Publishing* (Alfred A. Knopf, 2015). McGrath is a former editor of the *New York Times Book Review* and a former journalist with *The New Yorker*.
2. Bennett Cerf, *At Random: The Reminiscences of Bennett Cerf* (Random House, 1977).

CHAPTER 4: WHOSE BOOK IS THIS?

1. Sigmund Freud, "O escritor e a fantasia," in *Obras completas volume 8: O delírio e os sonhos na Gradiva e outros textos* (1906–1909), trans. Paulo César de Souza (Companhia das Letras, 2015), 325–38.

CHAPTER 5: HIS MAJESTY, SILENCE

1. Jean Stein, "William Faulkner, the Art of Fiction No. 12," *The Paris Review*, no. 12 (Spring 1965).
2. Carvel Collins, "Georges Simenon, the Art of Fiction No. 9," *The Paris Review*, no. 9 (Summer 1955); Stein, "William Faulkner."
3. Marcílio França Castro, *O último dos copistas* (Companhia das Letras, 2024), 27.
4. Karl Kraus, *Aforismos*, trans. Renato Zwick (Arquipélago, 2019), 66. (Translated for the purposes of this book by Alison Entrekin.)

CHAPTER 6: AMOS

1. Carl Seelig, *Walks with Walser*, trans. Anne Posten (New Directions, 2017).

CHAPTER 7: HOW IT ALL BEGINS

1. Marion Capron, "Dorothy Parker, the Art of Fiction No. 13," *The Paris Review*, no. 13 (Summer 1956).
2. José Saramago, *Cadernos de Lanzarote I* (Companhia das Letras, 1997), 238. (Translated for the purposes of this book by Alison Entrekin.)
3. Saramago, *Cadernos de Lanzarote I*, 498.
4. Saramago, *Cadernos de Lanzarote I*, 287.
5. Gordon Lloyd Harper, "Saul Bellow, the Art of Fiction No. 37," *The Paris Review*, no. 36 (Winter 1966).
6. George Plimpton, "Ernest Hemingway, the Art of Fiction No. 21," *The Paris Review*, no. 18 (Spring 1958).

7. Ricardo Piglia, *The Diaries of Emilio Renzi: Formative Years*, trans. Robert Croll (Restless Books, 2017), 311.
8. Edward W. Said, *Beginnings: Intention and Method* (Columbia University Press, 1985).
9. Amos Oz, *The Story Begins: Essays on Literature*, trans. Maggie Bar-Tura (Harcourt Brace, 1999), 2.
10. Oz, *The Story Begins*, 6.
11. Franz Kafka, *The Metamorphosis*, trans. Susan Bernofsky (W. W. Norton, 2014).
12. Oz, *The Story Begins*, 3.
13. Albert Camus, *The Stranger*, trans. Matthew Ward (Vintage International, 2012), 3.
14. Oz, *The Story Begins*, 8.
15. Julio Cortázar, *Hopscotch*, trans. Gregory Rabassa (Random House, 2020).

CHAPTER 8: HOW FAR CAN WE GO?

1. Carlo Ginzburg, *Clues, Myths, and the Historical Method*, trans. John and Anne C. Tedeschi (Johns Hopkins University Press, 2013).
2. Milan Kundera, *The Art of the Novel*, trans. Linda Asher (Grove Press, 1988), 13.
3. Kundera, *The Art of the Novel*, 40.
4. Luiz Schwarcz, *The Absent Moon: A Memoir of a Short Childhood and a Long Depression*, trans. Eric Becker (Penguin Press, 2023).
5. A. Scott Berg, *Max Perkins: Editor of Genius* (Berkley Books, 2008).
6. Raymond Carver, *Raymond Carver: Collected Stories* (Random House, 2009).

CHAPTER 9: OLIVER

1. Messerschmidt's sculptures are in the Belvedere museum in Vienna.

CHAPTER 10: PRIDE AND POWER

1. Berg, *Max Perkins*, 14.
2. His first text, *Lenita*, was coauthored and wasn't considered by Amado to be part of his oeuvre.
3. Laurence Hallewell, *O livro no Brasil: Sua história*, trans. Maria da Penha Villalobos, Lólio Lourenço de Oliveira, and Geraldo Gerson de Souza (Edusp, 2017), 467. (Translated for the purposes of this book by Alison Entrekin.)
4. Many authors dissatisfied with Schmidt would move to the publishing house Ariel.
5. Sam Jordison, "Bogged Down on Swann's Way?," *The Guardian*, February 7, 2013, theguardian.com/books/2013/feb/07/reading-group-swanns-way.
6. Alison Flood, "'It Needs More Public-Spirited Pigs': TS Eliot's Rejection of Orwell's Animal Farm," *The Guardian*, May 26, 2016, theguardian.com/books/2016/may/26/ts-eliot-rejection-george-orwell-animal-farm-british-library-online.
7. "Famous Authors' Harshest Rejection Letters," *Flavorwire*, November 17, 2011, flavorwire.com/232203/famous-authors-harshest-rejection-letters.
8. Eric Colleary, "How 'The Diary of Anne Frank' First Made It to the U.S.," *Time*, October 24, 2015, time.com/4081483/how-the-diary-of-anne-frank-first-made-it-to-the-u-s; the Doubleday editor Judith Jones was responsible for rescuing

Anne Frank's original manuscript from the slush pile and getting it published.

9. "Vladimir Nabokov: Lolita First Published in US 52 Years Ago," *Reader's Almanac* (blog), Library of America, August 18, 2010, blog.loa.org/2010/08/vladimir-nabokov-lolita-first-published.html.
10. Alice Vincent, "The Rejection Letters: How Publishers Snubbed 11 Great Authors," *The Telegraph*, June 5, 2014, telegraph.co.uk/culture/books/booknews/10877825/The-rejection-letters-how-publishers-snubbed-11-great-authors.html.
11. Emily Temple, "'Perhaps We're Being Dense.' Rejection Letters Sent to Famous Writers," *Literary Hub*, June 19, 2019, lithub.com/perhaps-were-being-dense-rejection-letters-sent-to-famous-writers.
12. Temple, "'Perhaps We're Being Dense.'"
13. The letter from editor Alfred C. Fifield to Gertrude Stein can be read in "Gertrude Stein Gets a Snarky Rejection Letter from Publisher (1912)," *Open Culture*, June 27, 2013, openculture.com/2013/06/gertrude_stein_a_snarky_rejection_letter_from_publisher_1912.html.
14. A play on the famous line by Che Guevara: "You must toughen up, but without ever losing your tenderness."

CHAPTER 11: JAMES JOYCE MEETS ADELAIDE CARRARO

1. Kevin Birmingham, *The Most Dangerous Book: The Battle for James Joyce's Ulysses* (Penguin, 2014), 62. (The exact phrase is "when he beat a German's brains out.")
2. Bennett Cerf, *At Random: The Reminiscences of Bennett Cerf* (Random House, 1977).

CHAPTER 13: THE WRITER ONSTAGE

1. Fernando Pessoa, *A Little Larger Than the Entire Universe: Selected Poems*, trans. Richard Zenith (Penguin, 2006), 3.
2. Fyodor Dostoevsky, *The Idiot*, trans. Eva Martin (Open Road Media, 2020), x.
3. Fyodor Dostoevsky, *Crime and Punishment*, trans. Richard Pevear and Larissa Volokhonsky (Vintage Classics, 1992), 233.
4. Thomas Bernhard, *Gathering Evidence*, trans. David McLintock (Alfred A. Knopf, 1985), 161.
5. Bernhard, *Gathering Evidence*, 159.
6. Bernhard, *Gathering Evidence*, 161.
7. Bernhard, *Gathering Evidence*, 209. Translator's note: The line "and I was a theater manager from a very young age" is not present in the Knopf edition and was translated into English from the Brazilian edition: *Origem*, trans. Sergio Tellaroli (Companhia das Letras, 2006), 311–12.
8. Fyodor Dostoevsky, *Demons*, trans. Larissa Volokhonsky and Richard Pevear (Aegitas, 2018), x.
9. Vasily Grossman, *Life and Fate*, trans. Robert Chandler (Journal Press, 2019).
10. Grossman, *Life and Fate*, 25.
11. Vasily Grossman, *Vida e destino*, trans. Irineu Franco Perpetuo (Alfaguara, 2014), 9.

CHAPTER 15: THE WAIT

1. Karl Ove Knausgård, *Dancing in the Dark*, trans. Don Bartlett (Archipelago Books, 2015).
2. Knausgård, *Dancing in the Dark*, 473–74.

BIBLIOGRAPHY

Berg, A. Scott. *Max Perkins: Editor of Genius*. Berkley Books, 2008.

Bernhard, Thomas. *Gathering Evidence*. Translated by David McLintock. Alfred A. Knopf, 1985.

Birmingham, Kevin. *The Most Dangerous Book: The Battle for James Joyce's Ulysses*. Penguin, 2014.

Camus, Albert. *The Stranger*. Translated by Matthew Ward. Vintage International, 2012.

Capron, Marion. "Dorothy Parker, the Art of Fiction No. 13." *The Paris Review*, no. 13 (Summer 1956). theparisreview.org/interviews/4933/the-art-of-fiction-no-13-dorothy-parker.

Carver, Raymond. *Raymond Carver: Collected Stories*. Random House, 2018.

Castro, Marcílio França. *O último dos copistas*. Companhia das Letras, 2024.

Cerf, Bennett. *At Random: The Reminiscences of Bennett Cerf*. Random House, 1977.

Collins, Carvel. "Georges Simenon, The Art of Fiction No. 9." *The Paris Review*, no. 9 (Summer 1955). theparisreview.org/interviews/5020/the-art-of-fiction-no-9-georges-simenon.

Cortázar, Julio. *Hopscotch*. Translated by Gregory Rabassa. Random House, 2020.

Dostoevsky, Fyodor. *Crime and Punishment*. Translated by Richard Pevear and Larissa Volokhonsky. Vintage Classics, 1992.

———. *The Idiot*. Translated by Eva Martin. Open Road Media, 2020.

"Famous Authors' Harshest Rejection Letters." *Flavorwire*, November 17, 2011. flavorwire.com/232203/famous-authors-harshest-rejection-letters.

Flood, Alison. "'It Needs More Public-Spirited Pigs': TS Eliot's Rejection of Orwell's Animal Farm." *The Guardian*, May 26, 2016. theguardian.com/books/2016/may/26/ts-eliot-rejection-george-orwell-animal-farm-british-library-online.

Freud, Sigmund. "O escritor e a fantasia." In *Obras completas volume 8: O delírio e os sonhos na Gradiva e outros textos (1906–1909)*. Translated by Paulo César de Souza. Companhia das Letras, 2015.

"Gertrude Stein Gets a Snarky Rejection Letter from Publisher (1912)." Open Culture, June 27, 2013. openculture.com/2013/06/gertrude_stein_a_snarky_rejection_letter_from_publisher_1912.html.

Ginzburg, Carlo. *Clues, Myths, and the Historical Method*. Translated by John and Anne C. Tedeschi. Johns Hopkins University Press, 2013.

Grossman, Vasily. *Life and Fate*. Translated by Robert Chandler. Journal Press, 2019.

Hallewell, Laurence. *O livro no Brasil: Sua história*. Translated by Maria da Penha Villalobos, Lólio Lourenço de Oliveira, and Geraldo Gerson de Souza. Edusp, 2017.

Harper, Gordon Lloyd. "Saul Bellow, the Art of Fiction No. 37." *The Paris Review*, no. 36 (Winter 1966). theparisreview.org/interviews/4405/the-art-of-fiction-no-37-saul-bellow.

Kafka, Franz. *The Metamorphosis*. Translated by Susan Bernofsky. W. W. Norton, 2014.

Knausgård, Karl Ove. *Dancing in the Dark*. Translated by Don Bartlett. Archipelago Books, 2015.

Kraus, Karl. *Aforismos*. Translated by Renato Zwick. Arquipélago, 2019.

Kundera, Milan. *The Art of the Novel*. Translated by Linda Asher. Grove Press, 1988.

McGrath, Charles. Introduction to *Alfred A. Knopf, 1915–2015: A Century of Publishing*. Knopf, 2015.

Oz, Amos. *The Story Begins: Essays on Literature*. Translated by Maggie Bar-Tura. Harcourt Brace, 1999.

Pessoa, Fernando. *A Little Larger Than the Entire Universe: Selected Poems*. Translated by Richard Zenith. Penguin, 2006.

Piglia, Ricardo. *The Diaries of Emilio Renzi: Formative Years*. Translated by Robert Croll. Restless Books, 2017.

———. *O último leitor*. Translated by Heloisa Jahn. Companhia das Letras, 2006.

Plimpton, George. "Ernest Hemingway, the Art of Fiction No. 21." *The Paris Review*, no. 18 (Spring 1958). theparisreview.org/interviews/4825/the-art-of-fiction-no-21-ernest-hemingway.

Said, Edward W. *Beginnings: Intention and Method*. Columbia University Press, 1985.

Saramago, José. *Cadernos de Lanzarote I*. Companhia das Letras, 1997.

Seelig, Carl. *Walks with Walser*. Translated by Anne Posten. New Directions, 2017.

Stein, Jean. "William Faulkner, the Art of Fiction No. 12." *The Paris Review*, no. 12 (Spring 1965). theparisreview.org/interviews/4954/the-art-of-fiction-no-12-william-faulkner.

Temple, Emily. "'Perhaps We're Being Dense.' Rejection Letters Sent to Famous Writers." *Literary Hub*, June 19, 2019. lithub.com/perhaps-were-being-dense-rejection-letters-sent-to-famous-writers.

Vincent, Alice. "The Rejection Letters: How Publishers Snubbed 11 Great Authors." *The Telegraph*, June 5, 2014. telegraph.co.uk/culture/books/booknews/10877825/The-rejection-letters-how-publishers-snubbed-11-great-authors.html.

"Vladimir Nabokov: Lolita First Published in U.S. 52 Years Ago." *Reader's Almanac* (blog). Library of America, August 18, 2010. blog.loa.org/2010/08/vladimir-nabokov-lolita-first-published.html.

INDEX